D1434013

WITHDRAWN

Dictionary of

CITY OF LONDON
STREET NAMES

Dictionary of

CITY
OF LONDON
STREET NAMES

AL SMITH

DAVID & CHARLES : *Newton Abbot*

7153 4880 9

*Set in 11 on 12 point Baskerville
and printed in Great Britain
by Latimer Trend & Company Limited Plymouth
for David & Charles (Publishers) Limited
South Devon House Newton Abbot Devon*

Contents

List of Illustrations

Introduction

As a taxi-driver the famous historic buildings and streets of London form part of my working day. Questions asked of me by tourists prompted me to learn more about London's history, and many of my lunch hours have been spent doing research, either in the ancient Guildhall Library, or in the reference library in my own town of Enfield. My interest in London's history has brought me into contact with many foreign visitors, and, during the course of a tour, I have often been asked the origin of a particular street name. Several books have been published on this subject but most of these were written in the nineteenth century; London has seen two world wars since then, and because of the heavy bombing in World War II is very much altered.

The City of London, of course, is the original London, and the streets in the City have been constructed over a period of nearly 2,000 years, the majority still bearing their original titles. My research into their origin has revealed streets and alleyways that I never knew existed, many of them hidden between huge office blocks which were built by the Victorians who seemed to have little regard for the City's historical lay-out. But London has withstood the indifference of the Victorians and the bombs of Hitler, and the streets and buildings of the City still bear witness to its historic past.

Dictionary of Street Names

ABCHURCH LANE EC4 (Cornhill to Cannon Street) F4

The lane takes its name from the church of St Mary Abchurch which stands at the Cannon Street end of the lane. The derivation of the name Abchurch is uncertain. It is thought that the original title was Upchurch, ie built on rising ground; the church does stand on the southern slopes of Cornhill. The prefix Ab could easily have come from *Aba*, a very common Saxon family name, perhaps that of the builders of the first church.

The church founded in the twelfth century was completely destroyed in the Great Fire of London in 1666 and was rebuilt by Wren in 1686. The cupola was painted by William Snow; the font and other woodwork is by Grinling Gibbons. On 8 September 1940 the southern end of the church was hit and partially destroyed by a German bomb, wrecking much of the work of these fine craftsmen, but disclosing the original flagstone floor with its inset gravestones. The church has now been restored to its original condition by Godfrey Allen, and is considered to be one of the most beautiful in the City.

ADAMS COURT EC2 (Old Broad Street) F3

Derives its name from the house of the abbots of St Albans which stood here in the fifteenth century. Adams being a corruption of St Albans.

ADDLE HILL EC4 (Carter Lane to Knightrider Street) C4

The name originated in Saxon times, either because the hill was the property of King Adelstan (Athelstan) or from the

11

Saxon word *adel*, ie *noble*, a street occupied largely by Saxon nobility.

ADDLE STREET EC2 (Wood Street to Aldermanbury) D2
The palace of King Adelstan stood here in the tenth century, the street being recorded as King Adel Strete. According to Stow in his *Survey of London* there was still one square tower of the palace standing in the sixteenth century.

ALBION PLACE EC2 (London Wall) E2
Albion chapel, a Presbyterian chapel, was erected on the site of the Old Bethlehem or Bedlam hospital. The chapel was built for Scots living in London and was demolished in the late nineteenth century to make way for an office block.

ALDERMANBURY EC2 (Gresham Street) E2
The court or *bury* of the aldermen of the City stood here in the fourteenth century; it was the forerunner of the Guildhall, which was moved to its present site in 1411.

The church of St Mary Aldermanbury, rebuilt by Wren after the great fire, stood on the corner of Love Lane. The church was partially destroyed by the bombing of 1940, then shipped stone by stone to America where it has been re-erected to the original Wren specifications. The tomb of Judge Jeffreys, which lay in the church, was lost in the bombing.

In Aldermanbury Square stands the hall of the Brewers Company, built in 1960 to replace the seventeenth-century hall which was destroyed in the bombing of 1940.

ALDERMANS WALK EC2 (Bishopsgate) G2
In the seventeenth century the cottage of Alderman Francis Dashwood stood just outside the City wall. The little lane that led to his home was called Dashwoods Walk, but this was later changed to Aldermans Walk. Another member of the Dashwood family, Sir Samuel, was elected Lord Mayor of London in 1702.

ALDERSGATE STREET EC1 (St Martins le Grand to Goswell Road) D2

The street takes its name from the gate built in the City wall in the ninth century by a Saxon builder named Aldred or Aldrich. In early times the gate was called Aldredsgate then later became known as Aldrichgate. The gate was completely rebuilt in 1618 with a statue of James I standing above the central arch, commemorating the fact that he was the first Stuart king to enter the City via that gateway. The gate was demolished in 1761 and a plaque on the wall of the building just north of Gresham Street marks its site.

A little farther along the street on the western side stands the church of St Botolph, which was built in 1788 by Nathaniel Wright. In the churchyard stands a statue of Sir Robert Peel, founder of the City's police force and from whom they earned their early nickname *peelers*. Part of the churchyard is used by postmen from the nearby General Post Office seeking peace and quiet and has been named Postmans' Park. In a cloister in the park is an interesting display of tablets commemorating acts of heroism, especially the saving of human life.

In the sixteenth century Aldersgate Street was largely occupied by nobility. Here stood the mansions of the Earls of Westmorland, the Duke of Northumberland, and the Earl of Shaftesbury, all being remembered in the names of courtways and office blocks. William Shakespeare is believed to have lived in number 134.

The street was very badly bombed in 1940. On the eastern side large skyscraper office blocks are being erected as part of the Barbican redevelopment scheme.

ALDGATE EC3 (eastern end of Fenchurch Street) H3

Named after the gate which spanned the road between Dukes Place and Jewry Street. Aldgate, or the Saxon *Aelgate*, means *open to all*, a free gate; it was one of the four original gates in the City wall. The old Roman road to Colchester, now known as Whitechapel Road, ran eastwards from it.

Geoffrey Chaucer, the author and poet, leased the dwelling above the gate in 1374, and Queen Mary I rode in triumph through it after being proclaimed Queen of England in 1553. In 1609 a new gate was erected with a statue of James I, the reigning monarch, beside it, but this gate was demolished in 1761.

Aldgate pump, a famous London landmark, stands on the site of a communal well, believed to have belonged to an old Saxon church called St Michael's, which was demolished in 1108 to make way for the building of the priory of Holy Trinity.

ALLHALLOWS LANE EC4 (Upper Thames Street) E4

Takes its name from the church of All Hallows the Great which stood on the corner of Upper Thames Street. The church, rebuilt by Wren after the Great Fire of 1666, was sometimes called All Hallows in the Ropery because it stood in an area where London's ropemakers lived. The great steelyard of the German Hanseatic League stood next to All Hallows Lane, the German steelworkers using the church as their own. The Hanse, or Easterlings, were a band of German steel merchants who completely dominated the European steel trade. It is said that from Easterlings has come the monetary term of sterling.

The church of All Hallows the Great was demolished in 1876 for the widening of Upper Thames Street, but part of the old tower can still be seen a little to the east of Cannon Street Station.

AMEN COURT EC4 (Warwick Lane) C3

In early days, before the Reformation, it was the custom of the clergy of St Paul's to walk in procession round the cathedral chanting the 'Our Father' in Paternoster Row, the 'Hail Mary' in Ave Maria Lane, and the 'Amen' in Amen Court or Corner. Whilst the procession was in progress the

'Credo' was chanted on the corner of Creed Lane. The old Roman wall runs beneath the buildings at the western end of the court. Some eighteenth-century houses still stand, their wrought-iron gates complete with the old lamp-lighters' trumpet-shaped snuffers.

AMERICA SQUARE EC3 (Crosswall) H4
The square, built about 1760, was dedicated to the American colonies. In the nineteenth century Baron Meyer de Roths-child lived at number 14. The square was bombed in 1941 and the house was demolished.

ANDREWS CROSS WC2 (Chancery Lane) A3
Takes its name from a sixteenth-century tavern standing in Chancery Lane. The tavern obviously catered for Scots living in London, the sign being the cross of St Andrew.

ANGEL COURT EC2 (Throgmorton Street) F3
In the Middle Ages Angel Court was a residential cul-de-sac with an inn called the Angel standing on the corner. In the court now stands Birch's restaurant, a favourite lunchtime rendezvous in the City, which originally stood in Cornhill. In the reign of George I the restaurant was owned by Lucas Birch whose son, Samuel, became Lord Mayor in 1840. The restaurant was demolished in the 1920s, the old shop front being preserved in the Victoria and Albert Museum.

ARTHUR STREET EC4 (King William Street) F4
The derivation of the name of this street is uncertain, but it could perpetuate the name of Sir George Arthur (1784–1854), a soldier who served his country in the war against Napoleon and was later made Lieutenant-General of Upper Canada. Or perhaps the architect of London Bridge, James Rennie, remembering his native Scotland, named it after the hill just outside Edinburgh, called Arthur's Seat.

ARTILLERY LANE E1 (Bishopsgate) G2

In 1585 fear of a Spanish Armada and war with Spain was uppermost in the minds of the City aldermen. Trained bands of Londoners were marshalled for practice on the artillery ground near Bishopgate Street. Here the Tower gunners fired their cannon-balls at earthen butts. The approach lane to the artillery ground was called Teasel Close but its name was changed to Artillery Lane. Later, in 1622, the practice ground was moved to Finsbury, where it still stands—known as the Honourable Artillery Company grounds.

ARTIZAN STREET E1 (Stoney Lane) H3

New industrial dwellings for skilled workers or artisans were erected here in the late nineteenth century.

ASHENTREE COURT EC4 (Whitefriars Street) B3

In the fourteenth century there stood in the gardens of the Carmelite convent a huge ash, which gave its name to the court.

AUSTIN FRIARS EC2 (Old Broad Street) F3

The name is a corruption of Augustinian Friars, a priory founded in 1243 by Humphrey de Bohun, Earl of Essex. At the dissolution of the monasteries Henry VIII gave the priory to William Powlett, the Marquis of Winchester, who erected a house on the site called Winchester House. The church in the priory, however, was retained by the king, who gave it to his son, Edward VI. In 1550 Edward VI gave the church to the Dutch nation, and it has been known as the Dutch church ever since. The church was badly bombed in 1940, but was completely restored in 1954.

AVE MARIA LANE EC4 (Ludgate Hill) C3

The 'Hail Mary' in the procession of the clergy of St Paul's cathedral was chanted in this lane (see Amen Court) during the ceremonial walk round the cathedral. During Queen

Page 17 (above) Watling Street, the oldest street in the City, with St Paul's in the background; (below) entrance to St Bartholomew the Great, the oldest church in the City

Page 18 St Martin's le Grand, with St Paul's in the background, in 1760

Anne's reign the Black Boy coffee house, standing in this lane, was famous for the sale and auction of books, and was a meeting place for authors and publishers.

BALES COURT EC4 (Old Bailey) C3
Peter Bales was one of the most famous calligraphers in England during the reign of Queen Elizabeth I. He ran a school for handwriting and shorthand in Old Bailey, in the court that perpetuates his name.

BARBICAN EC1 (Aldersgate Street) D1
A Roman tower (*barbicana*) stood just north of the street that bears its name. The Saxons gave it a name, *burgh kennin* or *town watch*tower. Fires were lit on top of the tower to guide travellers through the hills of Hampstead and Highgate to the city gates.

The City records show that in the early fourteenth century the care and upkeep of the tower or *burgh kennin* was given to the Earl of Suffolk.

The area was completely destroyed in the first air raid on London in 1940. Whole streets have disappeared; Jewin Street (the Jews' burial ground), Redcross Street, Monkwell Street and Harp Street, have gone for ever; large office blocks are being built on their ruins.

John Milton lived in the Barbican in 1647.

BARNARDS INN EC1 (Holborn) A2
Formerly Mackworths Inn, named after John Mackworth, Dean of Lincoln, it was leased in 1450 to Lionel Barnard, the principal of the Inn of Chancery, whose name the Inn adopted. The Inn was almost destroyed in the anti-Catholic (Gordon) riots of 1780, when homes of Catholics living near by were set on fire.

BARTHOLOMEW CLOSE EC1 (Little Britain) C2
Takes its name from the ancient priory of St Bartholomew

B 19

which occupied this site. All that remains of the priory, founded by Rahere the court jester to Henry I, is the church of St Bartholomew the Great. The present church is really only the choir and nave of the original church, which was destroyed by Henry VIII. The church was greatly restored by Prior Bolton in 1520; the rebus of Prior Bolton, a crossbow bolt piercing a tun or barrel, can be seen in the church.

In Bartholomew Close is the hall of the Butchers' Company, which was incorporated in 1606 but existed as early as the twelfth century.

BARTHOLOMEW LANE EC2 (Threadneedle Street) F3
Takes its name from the church that stood here called St Bartholomew by the Exchange which was demolished in 1841 to make way for the Sun Alliance Insurance building.

BARTLETT COURT EC4 (New Fetter Lane) B2
Thomas Bartlett, Edward VI's printer, lived and worked here; Bartlett was also the landlord of the Plow in Fetter Lane, a famous inn of the sixteenth century.

BASINGHALL STREET EC2 (Gresham Street) E3
Named after a rich city family called Basing, whose mansion stood at the southern end of the street. *Hawe* being Old English for enclosure, the whole ward was called Bassishaw, or Basing Hawe Ward. Adam Basing was Lord Mayor of London in 1251.

The street originally contained four City livery companies: Masons, Weavers, Coopers and Girdlers. Alas, after the bombing of 1941 only the Girdlers' Hall still stands. The whole area was devastated and on rebuilding the course of the street was slightly altered; so although the Hall was rebuilt on the site it has occupied for 600 years it now stands in Basinghall Avenue. The making of girdles or belts is no longer an art, but the company still has the honour of making the girdle and royal stole worn at coronations.

BEAR ALLEY EC4 (Farringdon Street) B3

In the seventeenth century an inn called the Beare stood in West Smithfield just to the north of the alley to which it gave its name.

BEECH STREET EC1 (Barbican) D1

Named after Nicholas de la Beche who was Lieutenant of the Tower of London in the fourteenth century, during the reign of Edward III. Prince Rupert, that famous soldier, lived in Beech Street in Drury House, named after its former owner Sir Drew Drury, who also gave his name to Drury Lane. The parish records show that Charles II visited Prince Rupert at this house, and that the bellringers were each given one guinea by the parish clerk for ringing the bells that heralded the king's arrival.

BEEHIVE PASSAGE EC3 (Lime Street) F4

Another of London's famous old taverns, the Beehive, stood on this site, and is remembered in the name.

BELL INN YARD EC3 (Gracechurch Street) F4

The Bell, one of London's most celebrated inns, stood at the end of this yard. Records show that the inn dates back to the early fourteenth century, when one William Dalby took its lease for three years at an annual rent of ten pounds. A City of London plaque marks the exact position of the Bell, stating that it was destroyed in 1666 in the Great Fire of London.

BELL WHARF LANE EC4 (Upper Thames Street) E4

This lane stands on the site of a more famous Thameside wharf, Three Cranes Wharf, so named because three huge beams used for lifting the wine casks shipped from Bordeaux stood here (see Queen Street Place). It was in a warehouse in Three Cranes Lane that Elizabeth Cromwell, wife of Oliver Cromwell, stored the royal possessions that she had stolen from Whitehall Palace, seventeen cartloads in all. A tavern called the Three Cranes was one of the most famous of all riverside inns.

Bell Wharf Lane originally stood a little farther to the east and was probably so named because it housed the warning bell for shipping. The whole area has now been demolished to make way for a City of London cleansing depot.

BELL YARD EC4 (Carter Lane) C3
An inn called the Bell stood here as late as the early eighteenth century; the old inn sign 'The Bell 1668' is now in the Guildhall Museum. William Shakespeare often dined at the Bell, perhaps discussing his plays with the locals.

BELL YARD WC2 (Fleet Street) A3
A sixteenth-century tavern called Le Belle stood in this yard, which was described by Alexander Pope, the eighteenth-century London poet, as one of Fleet Street's dirtiest little alleys.

BENETS HILL EC4 (Queen Victoria Street) C4
The church of St Benet Paul's Wharf stands in this street. It was founded in the early twelfth century, destroyed in the Great Fire of 1666, and rebuilt by Sir Christopher Wren in 1677–85. Here was buried Inigo Jones, the famous architect on 26 June 1652, aged eighty; his tomb and a monument to him were lost in the Great Fire. Here also are buried famous members of the nearby Heralds College. The church was handed over to the Welsh in London in 1879, and has since been known as the Welsh church.

Before Queen Victoria Street was built in 1871 the hill, which takes its name from this church, ran right through to Knightrider Street.

BEVIS MARKS EC3 (Camomile Street) G3
The name is a corruption of Buries Marks, the mark or site

of the mansion of the abbots of Bury St Edmunds in Suffolk, which stood here in the twelfth century. In the early sixteenth century the mansion became the property of Thomas Heneage. Nearby Heneage Lane perpetuates his name.

On the north side of the street stood the Papey, a religious house founded in 1420, its members being professional mourners. A church dedicated to St Augustine, called St Augustine in the Wall, was given to the Fraternity of the Papey in the early fifteenth century and was converted into a house for poor priests. This house was later occupied by Sir Francis Walsingham, secretary to Queen Elizabeth I. The Roman wall ran along the northern side of this street, and parts of it are to be found in the foundations of houses on that side.

BILLITER STREET EC3 (Fenchurch Street) G4
This street in the early thirteenth century was called Belzeterlane, the street in which the belzeters or bellfounders lived and worked; as there were over 100 churches in the City at this time, the bellfounders had plenty to do.

BIRCHIN LANE EC3 (Lombard Street) F4
Birchin is a corruption of Birchouer, the name of a former owner of property in this street.

In the Middle Ages the street was famous for its cockney fripperers, or secondhand-clothes merchants, who had their stalls in Birchouer Lane and along the sides of Lombard Street.

In the eighteenth century one of London's most famous rendezvous for City merchants, Tom's Coffee House, stood in Birchin Lane.

BIRD IN HAND COURT EC2 (Poultry) E3
Possibly the site of a fifteenth-century tavern of this name, well suited for the poultry end of the great West Cheap (Cheapside) Market.

BISHOPSGATE EC2 (Cornhill to Norton Folgate) G2

One of the longest streets in the City, it takes its name from the gate which spanned the City wall at a point where Camomile Street and Wormwood Street meet at the junction of Bishopsgate. The gate acquired its name from its reputed builder, a Saxon bishop of London called Erkenwald, and because of this the bishops of London received one stick from every cart laden with wood that passed through it. The Bishop's Gate was built a little to the west of the original Roman gate; then, in 1479, during the reign of Edward IV, a new gate was erected by the Hanse merchants who came from the great German steelyard in Upper Thames Street.

Sir Thomas Gresham built his house in Bishopsgate in 1563, the house occupying the whole area between Bishopsgate and Old Broad Street. This house was later converted into Gresham College, but was demolished in 1768. A modern office block, Gresham House, stands on the site. A little farther north stands the tiny fourteenth-century church of St Ethelburga; Ethelburga was a sister of Erkenwald, builder of Bishopsgate. Windows in the church commemorate Henry Hudson and his companions who received Holy Communion here before sailing to discover Hudson Bay in 1607. The front of this little church was hidden by shops which jutted into the road until they were demolished in 1933 as a traffic hazard.

A little farther north, after passing the site of the old gate, which was demolished in 1760, stands the church of St Botolph without Bishopsgate, the name denoting that the church stood outside the City gate. The present church was built in 1728 on the site of a much older building. The baptism of Edward Alleyn, founder of the Fortune theatre, is recorded here. There is also a monument to Sir Paul Pindar, wealthy City merchant, Ambassador to Turkey in 1611, who is buried in the church (see Pindar Street).

Opposite Liverpool Street station, which takes up most of

24

the northern end of Bishopsgate, stands one of London's most famous pubs, called Dirty Dicks (see Catherine Wheel Alley).

BLACKFRIARS BRIDGE EC4 (New Bridge Street) B4

London Bridge was the only bridge in the City spanning the Thames until Blackfriars Bridge was built in 1769. Robert Mylne, a young Scottish architect, won the competition to design the new bridge, which when first erected was named after William Pitt, the great minister of the day. Pitt Bridge later became Blackfriars Bridge in memory of the great Dominican monastery of the Black Friars which stood a little to the north of the bridge. In 1869 a new bridge was completed by Joseph Cubitt at a cost of £400,000, the opening ceremony being performed by Queen Victoria, whose statue stands at the northern end of the bridge.

Robert Mylne is buried in St Paul's cathedral near its own great architect, Sir Christopher Wren.

BLACKFRIARS LANE EC4 (*The Times*) C4

Blackfriars Lane occupies part of the site of the Dominican monastery of the Black Friars standing here between 1276 and 1538. The monastery became one of the most famous places in London. Charles V of France chose to stay here in 1522. Henry VIII held his Black Parliament here, and was granted a divorce from Katharine of Aragon by the jury of cardinals, who used the hall of the priory as their council chamber. The monastery was closed in 1538 by Henry VIII's dissolution of the monasteries. Parts of the old priory passed eventually into the hands of James Burbage, the actor, who founded the Blackfriars Theatre about 1596. Shakespeare, a friend of Burbage, purchased a house near by and frequently acted in the theatre, which was pulled down in 1655. *The Times* building occupies part of the site of the old monastery.

BLACK RAVEN ALLEY EC4 (Upper Thames Street) E5

The Black Raven inn stood on the corner of this alley and Upper Thames Street in the sixteenth century.

BLACK SWAN ALLEY EC2 (London Wall) E2

As late as 1750 a tavern called the Black Swan stood on the corner of London Wall.

BLOMFIELD STREET EC2 (London Wall) F2

The street is named after Lord Blomfield. Born in Bury St Edmunds in 1786 he became Bishop of London and a very effective speaker in the House of Lords on ecclesiastical subjects. At one time he was rector of the church of St Botolph without Bishopsgate. He died in Fulham Palace in 1857.

BOLT COURT EC4 (Fleet Street) B3

An inn called the Bolt in Tun once stood on the opposite side of Fleet Street, named after Prior Bolton who did so much to restore the church of St Bartholomew the Great in West Smithfield. Prior Bolton's rebus in that church shows a bolt (a crossbow arrow) passing through a tun (a beer cask). The Bolt in Tun was one of the last of London's coaching inns; at one time it despatched twenty-six coaches a day to the West Country. Dr Johnson, the famous writer, moved into 8 Bolt Court after the death of his wife, and stayed there until his death in 1784.

BOND COURT EC4 (Walbrook) E4

The court is named after Alderman William Bond of Walbrook Ward, who lived here in the seventeenth century. The Bond family had been connected with the administration of the City for two centuries. William Bond's father, also an alderman, purchased the famous Crosby Hall in 1566 and his family lived there for thirty years.

BOTOLPH LANE EC3 (Eastcheap) F4

The church of St Botolph Billingsgate at the foot of Botolph

Lane was destroyed in the fire of 1666 and was not rebuilt. Three of the City's old churches stood here almost touching one another: St Botolph Billingsgate, St George Billingsgate, and St Mary at Hill. Only St Mary at Hill survives, for though St George's was only damaged in the Great Fire of 1666, not destroyed like St Botolph's, and was rebuilt by Wren in 1674, it was finally demolished in 1895.

BOUVERIE STREET EC4 (Fleet Street) B3
The landlords of this site, which was once occupied by the thirteenth-century Whitefriars Priory, are the Pleydell Bouveries, Earls of Radnor. Most of the street today is taken up by the *News of the World* building. Pleydell Street stands at the Fleet Street end of Bouverie Street.

BOW LANE EC4 (Cheapside) D3
Bow Lane, once called Hosier Lane from the people of that trade living there, is now named after the church of St Mary le Bow, which has stood on this site from at least the twelfth century. The church is so named because it stands on bows or stone arches. It was the great bells of St Mary that were supposed to have called Dick Whittington back from High-gate Hill to become Lord Mayor of London in the fourteenth century. In the fifteenth century the Common Council decreed that the largest of Bow Bells should ring at 9 pm every evening to signify the closing time for shops. The church was totally destroyed in the Great Fire of 1666, but Sir Christopher Wren completed its rebuilding in 1680, giving it the finest spire of all his churches: a certain good lady named Dame Dyonis Williamson donated £2,000 towards the work.

The church was badly damaged by enemy action in 1941, but has since been completely restored. The twelve great bells, damaged in the bombing, have been melted down and recast. Standing in Bow churchyard is a statue of Captain John Smith (1580–1631) who was one of the first leaders of the settlement in Jamestown, Virginia.

Londoners say that anyone born within the sound of Bow Bells can claim to be a true cockney.

BRABANT COURT EC3 (Gracechurch Street) F4
The City contains within its boundaries branches of many of the world's banks, among them those of the Low Countries —Belgium and Holland. Brabant is one of the nine provinces of Belgium, the court is named after it; also, John, Duke of Brabant, lived near this site in the fourteenth century.

BRACKLEY STREET EC1 (Golden Lane) D1
In 1687 the house of the Earl of Bridgewater was burnt down, the Earl losing in the fire his two infant sons, Charles, Viscount Brackley, and the younger son Thomas. It was a famous tragedy of the times, and all the streets in the area are named in memory of the family—Bridgewater Square and Street, Viscount Street, and Brackley Street.

BREAD STREET EC4 (Queen Victoria Street) D4
In the year 1302 King Edward I decreed that no baker should sell bread from his own house or shop, but from the bread market to be formed in Bread Street.

John Milton, the poet and author of *Paradise Lost*, was born in Bread Street in 1608; he was baptised in the church of All Hallows, Bread Street, which stood on the corner of Watling Street. Wren rebuilt this church after the Great Fire, but it was condemned in 1877 and pulled down. Another of Wren's churches, called St Mildred's, which stood in Bread Street between Queen Victoria Street and Cannon Street, was totally destroyed in the bombing of 1941. The church contained fine woodwork by Grinling Gibbons and the church records included the marriage of Shelley, the poet, in 1816.

BRICK COURT EC2 (Middle Temple Lane) A3
This was the first brick building in the Temple. Oliver Gold-

smith lived here in 1768 when he wrote *She Stoops to Conquer*. He died in the court in 1774.

BRIDE LANE EC4 (New Bridge Street) B3
Bride Lane and Bride Court take their names from the nearby church of St Bride's, Fleet Street (see St Brides Avenue). In Bride Lane stands the St Bride's Institute, which contains a fine reference library, recreation rooms, and a swimming pool. At the Fleet Street end of Bride Lane stands the Punch Tavern, with its Pickwick Bar as a reminder of the Charles Dickens period.

BRIDEWELL PLACE EC4 (New Bridge Street) B3
The Saxons and Normans built castles on this site near the well of St Bride's church. Henry built the palace of Bridewell here in 1522 in preparation of the visit of Charles V of France, and lived in it with Katharine of Aragon. As the poor Queen awaited the verdict of the cardinals who sat opposite in Blackfriars monastery debating Henry's petition for divorce, she must have listened for their footsteps crossing the little wooden bridge over the River Fleet that connected Blackfriars to the palace. The Fleet ditch soon became polluted with the filth and garbage of people living upstream at Holborn, and Henry moved to Whitehall Palace. His son, Edward VI, gave the old palace to the City council, who converted it into a home for orphan boys—soon known as the Bridewell boys.

It was completely destroyed in the Great Fire of 1666, and in 1688 was rebuilt as the dreaded Bridewell prison. Here men and women prisoners were flogged unmercifully before a judge, the flogging only ceasing when the judge allowed a hammer to fall on to a wooden block: 'Oh knock, Sir Robert, pray knock,' was the oft-heard cry at Bridewell. The old prison was eventually demolished in 1864, much to the relief of Londoners.

BRIDGEWATER SQUARE EC1 (Barbican) D1

Bridgewater House, the mansion of the Earls of Bridgewater, covered the whole of the area between Barbican and Fann Street. It was burnt down in 1687, the Earl losing both his infant sons in the fire (see Brackley Street).

BRITTEN'S COURT EC4 (Whitefriar Street) B3

In the cellar of number 4 Britten's Court can be seen part of the old Carmelite priory that formerly covered the whole of this area. Applications to see this ancient relic must be made to the *News of the World*, Bouverie Street.

BROKEN WHARF EC4 (Upper Thames Street) D4

A dispute between the joint owners of this wharf, the Abbots of Chertsey and the Abbots of Hamme, which lasted forty years, allowed the wharf to fall into a state of decay; on its eventual collapse it was referred to by Londoners as the Broken Wharf. Standing beside it in the fourteenth century was a large stone house belonging to Edward III's brother, the Earl Marshal of England.

BUCKLERSBURY EC4 (Poultry) E4

The Italian family Buckerel came to London in the thirteenth century and settled in the street that perpetuates their name. Buckerel's *bury* or house stood near the Walbrook, and was called Barge House because of the barges that sailed along the river at the side of the house. The Buckerel family soon took an active part in the administration of the City. Thomas, Stephen, and Matthew were sheriffs of London between 1217 and 1255, and Andrew Buckerel was Lord Mayor on seven consecutive occasions between 1231 and 1237. The street in the sixteenth and seventeenth centuries was inhabited by grocers, druggists, and herbalists. Shakespeare's Falstaff refers to the street in *The Merry Wives of Windsor*: 'like women in men's apparel, and smell like Bucklersbury'.

BUDGE ROW EC4 (Queen Victoria Street) E4
Prior to the bombing of London, Budge Row ran between
Watling Street and Cannon Street. Here, in the thirteenth
century, lived furriers and skinners. Budgers were dealers in
lambskin fur.

BULLS HEAD PASSAGE EC3 (Gracechurch Street) F4
The narrow alleyway through which thousands of City
workers pass on their way to Leadenhall market takes its
name from the sixteenth-century inn called the Bulls Head.
Charles Dickens in *Pickwick Papers* mentions the Green
Dragon tavern, standing in Bulls Head Passage, as the
favourite tavern of Sam Weller.

BURGON STREET EC4 (Carter Lane) C3
The Rev John Burgon, vicar of St Mary's church, Oxford,
and later Dean of Chichester, was a frequent visitor with his
family to the church of St Bride, Fleet Street, which is
situated near by. The street is named in honour of Dean
Burgon.

BURY STREET EC3 (Bevis Marks) G3
A mansion belonging to the abbots of Bury St Edmunds
occupied this site in the twelfth century (see Bevis Marks).
   The synagogue standing between Bury Street and Bevis
Marks was built by Spanish and Portuguese Jews to dis-
tinguish themselves from the German Jews whose synagogue
stands, though badly bombed, a little lower down in Dukes
Place.

BUSH LANE EC4 (Cannon Street) E4
The lane takes its name from a rich City family named
Busche, who lived here in the early fourteenth century.
During the construction of nearby Cannon Street station
pieces of Roman tessellated pavement were found beneath
the eastern side of Bush Lane.

BYWARD STREET EC3 (Great Tower Street) G4

Takes its name from the Byward tower in the Tower of London. Byward is a corruption of by-word, the two words or password required to gain entry to the Tower. In Byward Street stands the church of All Hallows, Barking, which was founded by the nuns of Barking Abbey in AD 675. The present church, constructed in the twelfth and fifteenth centuries, was one of the few to escape the Great Fire in 1666. From its tower, in fact, Samuel Pepys watched and recorded the progress of the flames.

The church register records the marriage of John Quincy Adams, who later became the sixth president of the United States; also recorded is the baptism of William Penn (born on 23 October 1644), founder of Pennsylvania. Penn, born on Tower Hill, broke away from his family because of his Quaker beliefs. His father, Sir William Penn, was Commander-in-Chief of the Navy.

In the old churchyard, which was badly bombed, were the bodies of many who fell by the axe on Tower Green. Beneath the high altar is said to be the heart of Richard I, the Lionheart, although the French claim that it lies in the cathedral in Rouen.

The church was very nearly destroyed in the bombing of 1941, but has been restored to its original condition and still contains some Saxon stonework and a little of the woodcarving of Grinling Gibbons. In the crypt can be seen some original Roman pavement dating from AD 45. The pulpit is a relic of Wren's church of St Swithin, Cannon Street, which was totally destroyed in 1941.

CAMOMILE STREET EC3 (Bishopsgate) G3

The site of the old Roman wall runs along the northern side of Camomile Street, its remains lying in the foundations of the buildings on that side. In the twelfth and thirteenth centuries no buildings stood near the wall at this point, and the land was allowed to become overgrown with weeds, one of which was camomile, a weed of the chrysanthemum family which was used to make medicine and herbs sold in the nearby grass market (Gracechurch Street). In the early twentieth century a section of Roman wall, 40 ft long, was discovered during excavations on the northern side of Camomile Street. The old Bishop's gate spanned the Roman wall between Camomile Street and Wormwood Street, until it was demolished in 1760.

CANNON ALLEY EC4 (St Paul's churchyard) C3
Some of the canons of St Paul's cathedral lived in houses situated in this alley during the seventeenth century.

CANNON STREET EC4 (St Paul's churchyard to King William Street) D4–E3
In the Middle Ages Cannon Street was one of the most densely populated areas in the City. Here lived the candle-makers and wick chandlers, the street then being known as Candelwrichstrete. Through a series of name-shortenings and the cockney dialect the name was contracted to Cannon Street in the mid-seventeenth century.

In 1833 during the construction of London Bridge a section of Roman road about 16 ft wide was discovered, the road seeming to run in the direction of the 'London Stone', or millarium, the point from which all distances were measured in Roman times. The Stone, considered to be one of the City's oldest relics can be seen in the wall of the Bank of China, which stands near St Swithins Lane (see St Swithins Lane).

In the twelfth century, close by London Stone, lived London's first Lord Mayor, Henry Fitz Ailwyne, who held the position for twenty-four years from 1189 to 1212.

A host of little lanes and two churchyards were demolished to make way for Cannon Street station, erected in 1866. The churchyard of St Mary Bothaw and the churchyard of St John the Baptist were all that was left of these two churches, which were destroyed in the Fire of 1666 and not rebuilt. On the corner of Queen Street and Cannon Street stands the London Chamber of Commerce. The western end of Cannon Street was particularly badly hit during the bombing of London, as the newly built office blocks show.

On a wall on the eastern side of the lawns fronting Gateway House is a bust of Admiral Arthur Phillip, RN, commemorating the landing in Australia in 1788. Bronze murals depicting the actual landing were salvaged from the blitzed church of St Mildred in nearby Bread Street. Admiral Phillip was born in Bread Street.

On the wall of number 37 Cannon Street is a tablet marking the site of the first Salters Hall, built in 1454. On the corner of New Change a plaque marks the site of the Cordwainers' or Shoe Makers' Company which, before it was destroyed by bombs, stood at number 7 Cannon Street.

CAPEL COURT EC2 (Bartholomew Lane) F3

In Capel Court stood the house of Sir William Capel, Lord Mayor of London in 1503.

Capel Court is the official entrance to the Stock Exchange. In the late seventeenth century the Royal Exchange of Sir Thomas Gresham became a little too uncomfortably crowded for the jobbers and brokers of the Stock Exchange and a new site for business transactions was found in Change Alley, in the coffee houses of Jonathan's and Garraway's. In 1773 the jobbers changed the name of Jonathan's to the Stock Exchange. By the turn of the century these coffee houses were also becoming inadequate, and in 1801 the first stone of the present Stock Exchange was laid on the site of Mendoza's boxing rooms at Capel Court. In 1854 the Exchange was completely rebuilt from a design by Thomas Allason. Only members are admitted to the floor of the Stock Exchange, but the public are admitted to the Visitors' Gallery to see the Exchange in full operation.

Page 35 (*above*) St John's Gate 1969; (*below*) the site of Dryden's house, Fetter Lane

Page 36
Petticoat Lane in
the nineteenth
century

CAREY LANE EC2 (Gutter Lane) D3

The name is a corruption of Kirone Lane. A family named Kirone lived here in the thirteenth century, the name being contracted first from Kirone to Kyre and then to Carey.

CARMELITE STREET EC4 (Tudor Street) B4

Carmelite Street stands on part of the site of the thirteenth-century priory of the Carmelites or White Friars, which was founded by Sir Robert Gray. Modern Carmelite Street has been taken over by the world of journalism, as can be seen by the number of newspaper vans in the area. At the Tudor Street end is the City of London School for Girls, which was built in the early twentieth century.

CARTER LANE EC4 (Godliman Street) C3

The street takes its name from a fourteenth-century city merchant named Stephen le Charetter, who is recorded as living here in 1319. The seventeenth-century Harts Horn tavern which stood in Carter Lane was used as a rendezvous for the Guy Fawkes conspirators. Sir Christopher Wren leased a house in Carter Lane during the building of St Paul's cathedral. The St Paul's Chorister School occupies part of its northern side.

CARTHUSIAN STREET EC1 (Aldersgate Street) D1

Named after the Carthusian monastery which was founded in 1371 by Sir Walter de Manny as a memorial to the thousands of Londoners struck down by the Black Death. Many of the bodies of these victims are said to lie under Charterhouse Square, which is situated at the western end of Carthusian Street, outside the City boundary (see Charterhouse Street).

CASTLE BAYNARD WHARF EC4 (Upper Thames Street) C4

On the riverside at the site of this wharf stood a ten-towered castle and palace built in the eleventh century by Ralph Baynard, a nobleman of William the Conqueror. In the fifteenth century the castle was converted into a palace by Humphrey, Duke of Gloucester. In this palace in 1483 Richard III was offered the crown of England by the Duke of Buckingham after hearing the news of the death of the two princes in the Tower. Here also in 1553 the crown was offered to and accepted by Lady Jane Grey, the unfortunate queen who ruled for only nine days and subsequently lost her head on Tower Green. The palace was completely destroyed in the Great Fire of 1666 as it swept along the riverside.

CASTLE COURT EC3 (St Michael's Alley, Cornhill) F3
In Castle Court stands the George and Vulture, the favourite tavern of Charles Dickens, referred to in *Pickwick Papers*. The revived Pickwick Club met here, each member assuming the name of a Dickens character. Taverns have occupied this site for 600 years, the George and Vulture itself having twice been destroyed by fire. Coffee was first introduced to this tavern in the year 1652, and such was its popularity that part of the tavern was taken over as a coffee house. It is today one of the City's most popular eating-houses.

CASTLE YARD (Upper Thames Street) C4
The yard takes its name from Castle Baynard which occupied most of the riverfront a little to the west.

CATHEDRAL PLACE EC4 (Newgate Street) D3
This is now a large modern office block and shops which have been built on the site of several streets and alleyways destroyed in the bombing of 1941. Names so familiar to City workers before the bombing have gone for ever and are now only a memory: Paternoster Row, Ivy Lane, Paternoster Square, Rose Street, Queens Alley, and Lovells Court.

CATHERINE WHEEL ALLEY E1 (Middlesex Street) G2
Before the widening of Middlesex Street, Catherine Wheel

Alley ran through to Bishopsgate, emerging at the side of the famous old galleried coaching inn called the Catherine Wheel, which was destroyed by fire in 1895. Standing on almost the same site today is one of London's most famous pubs, Dirty Dicks. Dirty Dicks owes its name to Nathaniel Bentley, the son of a wealthy City merchant. Bentley inherited a large sum of money from his father with which he opened a shop in Leadenhall Street. He became engaged to a pretty young London lass, who died on the eve of the wedding. Bentley became a recluse, locking up his shop and leaving everything as it was on the day she died. The landlord of a pub in Bishopsgate bought up Bentley's possessions when he died—all the stock was covered in cobwebs and littered with the skeletons of rats and mice. The landlord displayed all these things in a museum in the pub, earning it the name of Dirty Dicks. The alley emerging at the side of the pub is now called Catherine Wheel Court.

CAVENDISH COURT EC3 (Houndsditch) G2
The house of the Earls of Devonshire whose family name is Cavendish stood on this site (see Devonshire Square).

CENTRAL MARKETS EC1 (Farringdon Street) C2
The Central Meat Market was opened in 1867 as the world's largest meat and provisions market. Three and a half million cartloads of earth were dug and carted away by hand to make way for the huge underground cold-storage stockrooms. The market was erected on the site of London's oldest livestock market, which was for centuries known as the King's Market, and reputed to be one of the dirtiest places in the City, ankle-deep in filth and mire. In 1615 an effort was made to clean it up by paving parts of it and constructing a form of sewer.

The cattle were led into the market by way of the old Cow Bridge which crossed the Fleet River. That Cow Bridge is now called Cowcross Street and the Fleet River has for a long time been covered over by Farringdon Road. By the middle of the nineteenth century the smell and filth and the screaming of slaughtered cattle became too much for the residents in the area, and on 11 June 1855 an order was made to remove the market to the Copenhagen Fields in Caledonian Road, Islington. The dead-meat market was transferred from Newgate Street to the Central Markets in 1868. The Caledonian Market is also closed now, but as late as 1956 vehicles driving down York Way in the early morning might be confronted by a herd of cattle or sheep being led along from Kings Cross station.

CHANCERY LANE WC2 (Fleet Street) A3

The earliest recorded name of this street is in the early thirteenth century when it was known as Newstrate. In 1233, during the reign of Henry III, a house was erected on the eastern side of the lane for the conversion of Jews to the Christian faith, each converted Jew receiving a payment of between a penny and twopence a day. The house of converts became a famous London landmark and Newstrate became Convers Lane.

Towards the end of the thirteenth century when Edward I ascended the throne he had cause to banish all Jews from the country, finding them guilty of debasing the coinage—clipping pieces off coins, melting them down, and casting new ones from the clippings, and in 1377 Edward III demolished the house of converts, erecting in its place an office for the Keeper of the Rolls (the official records of the courts and Inns of Chancery).

Once again the name of the street was changed, this time from Convers Lane to Chancellors Lane. For nearly 500 years the national records piled up, running into hundreds of thousands of rolls. Protests were made in the nineteenth century by historians and City officials at the difficulty experienced in the tracing of historical records. Eventually, in 1851 the Public Record Office was designed by Sir James

Pennethorne to stand on the site of the chapel of the old Rolls Office; it was completed in 1866, housing millions of public records. Some of its outstanding treasures today include the perfectly preserved Domesday Book, documents relating to the Gunpowder Plot and letters of the wives of Henry VIII. The building is of course open to the public on weekdays. A little to the south of the Public Records Office on the western side of Chancery Lane stands the Hall of the Law Society, which was built in 1830. Most of Chancery Lane lies outside the City boundary, only the Law Society and part of the Public Record Office being within it.

CHANGE ALLEY EC3 (Birchin Lane) F3
Named after the Royal Exchange, Change Alley became the centre of the stockbroking world in 1698 when jobbers and brokers moved from the overcrowded Exchange into the coffee houses in Change Alley. Thomas Garway, the first person to retail tea in England, around 1657, was the owner of Garraway's, one of the coffee houses frequented by the jobbers and brokers. This coffee house was destroyed by fire in 1748 and rebuilt, but was demolished in 1866 to make way for office blocks.

Jonathan's coffee house was the scene of the South Sea Bubble speculation in 1720 when the whole country seemed to gamble on the government-sponsored South Sea Company. The company, which was granted the exclusive right to trade with the South Sea islands, was started in 1711 by the Earl of Oxford, and was aided by the government in an effort to raise money to pay off the national debt. Despite warnings from Robert Walpole, thousands of people invested their savings in the venture, and when the 'bubble' burst wealthy men lost huge fortunes in a matter of minutes. The scenes in Change Alley were fantastic—brokers, jobbers, and investors spilled out into Cornhill demanding justice. The directors of the company were forbidden to leave the country and members of the government who were connected with it

41

were forced to resign. An inquiry showed that many false entries had been made in the company's books and that Members of Parliament had accepted bribes. The event was a world scandal, many men being ruined for life.

Jonathan's was demolished in the late nineteenth century to make way for the redesigning of Change Alley.

CHAPTER HOUSE COURT EC4 (St Paul's churchyard) C3
Before the bombing of the area around St Paul's churchyard there stood on the northern side of the churchyard the chapter house of St Paul's cathedral. Chapter House Court connected the churchyard with Paternoster Row, which was obliterated during the bombing of 1941. On the corner of Chapter House Court and Paternoster Row stood the celebrated Chapter Coffee House which was much frequented by famous authors and booksellers of the eighteenth century.

CHARTERHOUSE STREET EC1 (Farringdon Street) B2
This busy street, used by vehicles of the Central Meat Market, takes its name from the Carthusian Priory or *Chartreuse* which was founded in 1371 by Sir Walter de Manny with money left for the purpose by Michael de Northburgh, Bishop of London. The priory was erected on the site of the graveyard of some 50,000 victims of the Black Death of 1348, the graveyard then being known as Pardon Churchyard and standing outside the City wall. Today Charterhouse Square occupies the entire site. The priory existed for nearly 200 years until Henry VIII wreaked vengeance on the Church in 1536. John Houghton, last prior of Charterhouse was hung, drawn, and quartered at Tyburn for his defiance of Henry VIII; on 4 May 1535 his head was exhibited on London Bridge and his limbs were pinned to the gates of the priory.

The priory and lands passed into the hands of Sir Edward North, who built a fine house on the site. Queen Elizabeth I was entertained here in 1558 as a guest of Sir Edward. In 1565 the house was purchased by the Duke of Norfolk who enlarged it and called it Norfolk House. The duke was implicated in the plot of 1571 to put Mary Queen of Scots on the throne of England, and was beheaded for his part in the conspiracy. In 1611 Norfolk House was purchased by Thomas Sutton, a rich city merchant who founded Charterhouse School, which stood there until 1872 when it was moved to Godalming in Surrey. The site in Charterhouse Street was acquired by the Merchant Taylors Company, who used it as their school until 1935 when they also moved. The whole area was badly bombed in 1941, but part of the great cloister of the priory survived and the old Wash House Court has been restored.

During the summer months a tour of the Charterhouse can be arranged by application; a small fee is charged and a brochure on the priory is provided.

CHEAPSIDE EC2 (St Paul's churchyard) D3

It takes its name from the Anglo-Saxon *ceap*, to sell or barter. In the early eleventh century the street was the main market of the City, and was named West Cheap to distinguish it from another market near London Bridge called Eastcheap. Before the Great Fire of London, Cheapside was the most fashionable street and market in the City. At the western end, near St Paul's cathedral, in the middle of the street, stood the church of St Michael le Quern. In front of the church was a communal fountain called the Lesser Conduit, which was supplied with water drawn from the River Tyburn near modern Oxford Street; the water was piped through hollowed-out tree trunks.

At the corner of Wood Street stood the church of St Peter Cheap, the churchyard of which can still be seen hidden behind the shop standing on the corner of Wood Street. In the middle of the street, facing St Peter's church, was the great Cheapside Cross, one of the nine crosses erected by Edward I in honour of his dead Queen Eleanor. The cross was erected in 1290 and demolished in 1643. On the southern side of the street, between Bread Street and the church of St Mary le Bow, stood the huge gabled houses of the Goldsmiths Company—in Goldsmith's Row, built by Thomas Wood in 1491. Next to Goldsmith's Row stood the original church of St Mary le Bow (see Bow Lane).

In the middle of the road, opposite the church, stood the main water supply, called the Upper Conduit or Standard, which was also used as the site of some of the City's public executions. Next to Bow church stood the Crown Sild, a building erected in the fourteenth century by Edward III in order that he and his Queen, Philippa, could watch the jousting and pageants that took place in Cheapside (see Crown Court). In the middle of the road, fronting Old Jewry, stood the third and largest of the Cheapside conduits, called the Great Conduit. Cheapside was almost completely destroyed in the Great Fire of 1666. All three conduits melted in the heat, and three churches—St Michael le Quern, St Peter Cheap and St Mary le Bow—were destroyed, only St Mary le Bow being rebuilt.

Cheapside suffered badly again in the blitz of 1940–41, almost the whole of the southern side of the western end being destroyed. Friday Street, which formerly ran through to Cheapside, now terminates at Watling Street, and a Bank of England extension now occupies the whole of this devastated area. The church of St Mary le Bow was badly damaged, the restoration only recently being completed.

CHESHIRE COURT EC4 (Fleet Street) B3
Named after the famous City tavern called the Cheshire Cheese, the favourite haunt of journalists and American tourists. The tavern dates from the seventeenth century and stands in virtually the same surroundings as when Dr Johnson and Oliver Goldsmith visited it.

CHURCH ALLEY EC2 (Northern end of the Guildhall) E2
The alleyway formerly led to the parish church of St Michael

Bassishaw. The church was built in the twelfth century and was destroyed in the Great Fire, but was rebuilt by Wren. The church was demolished in 1899 to make way for Bassishaw House, which in turn was destroyed in the bombing of 1940–41.

CHURCH ENTRY EC4 (Carter Lane) C3
The passageway led to the church of St Anne, Blackfriars, which was built in the middle of the sixteenth century for the parishioners of Blackfriars. The church stood on the eastern side of the Blackfriars monastery and was destroyed in the Great Fire of 1666.

CIRCUS PLACE EC2 (Finsbury Circus) F2
Erected in 1850 to form an entrance to Finsbury Circus, one of the City's quiet retreats for office workers (see Finsbury Circus).

CLARKS PLACE EC2 (Bishopsgate) G3
In the late sixteenth century almshouses specially built for the parish clerks stood on this site.

CLEMENTS LANE EC4 (Lombard Street) F4
Named after the church of St Clement, Eastcheap, which stands at the southern end of the lane. Built in the early fourteenth century the church was destroyed in the Great Fire of 1666 and rebuilt by Wren in 1686. Henry Purcell, the great seventeenth-century composer, played the organ in St Clement's.

CLOAK LANE EC4 (Dowgate Hill) E4
Once called Horshew Bridge Street because it was shaped like a horseshoe with a little bridge at the eastern end that crossed the River Walbrook. The name Cloak is thought to be derived from the Latin *cloaca*, a sewer. The lane was probably a sewer running into the Walbrook.

45

CLOTH FAIR EC1 (Little Britain) C2

In the early twelfth century a fair lasting three days was held annually in this street to promote and publicise the woollen and drapery trades. Flemish and French weavers visited the fair, often lodging in the little street called Cloth Fair. The fair became one of the great events of London and by the seventeenth century had expanded to cover most of the area we know as West Smithfield. Charles II increased the duration of the fair to fourteen days. In Cloth Fair stood the Hand and Shears tavern where the Pie Powder or *Pied Poudre* court was held prior to the opening day of the fair for the inspection of weights and measures and for the granting of licences to sell goods.

By the eighteenth century the origins of the fair were forgotten; rope dancers, performing bears, gingerbread stalls, and the-fattest-man-in-the-world shows had taken its place. In the early nineteenth century mobs roamed the fair and women were assaulted, robbers and pickpockets were rife, and general fighting often led to abandonment of the festivities. One of the most notorious mobs was known as Lady Holland's gang. In the 1850s a move was made to end the fair and in 1855 it was finally closed; another of London's great fairs ended by mob rule and violence. Cloth Fair, Cloth Street, and Cloth Court all commemorate the original drapers' fair.

CLOTHIER STREET E1 (Cutler Street) G3

On Sunday mornings the Petticoat Lane market (see Middlesex Street) is one of the City's great attractions. The second-hand-clothes section of the market operated in this street and in 1906 it was named Clothier Street.

COCK LANE EC1 (Giltspur Street) C2

Cockfighting was the great sport of Englishmen in the seventeenth and eighteenth centuries. In Cock Lane were bred the fighting cocks for the City's cockpits. A good fighting cock weighed about 4½ lb and was fitted during combat with steel spurs called gaffles, which helped make the contest a little more gory. Cock Lane, one of the City's slums, was also a notorious brothel. The Great Fire of London started at Pudding Lane and finished at Pie Corner, the name given to the corner of Cock Lane and Giltspur Street, where in the seventeenth century stood the Fortune of War tavern. It was destroyed in the fire but the statue of a fat boy which adorned the front of the tavern was saved, and to this day can be seen on that corner, commemorating the finish of the Great Fire of London on 5 September 1666.

COLEMAN STREET EC2 (Gresham Street) E3

In AD 800 a *kohl mund* or cabbage patch was a gift to Bishop Alban from the Saxon king Egbert, and in medieval times the street built on the site of the *kohl mund* was inhabited by charcoal burners and coalmen. The derivation of the name is a conjecture based upon these two facts.

St Stephen, Coleman Street, a church rebuilt in 1676 by Wren on the site of the original twelfth-century church, stood at the southern end of the street on the western side; the church was used in 1665 as a burial ground for the victims of the great plague. A sexton of the church, John Hayward, personally collected the dead bodies from the narrow little alleyways off Coleman Street for burial in the churchyard: he was a famous figure in those days, with his handcart and bell and his call of 'bring out your dead'. The church was completely destroyed in the bombing of London in 1940–41. Somewhere beneath the modern office block erected on the site of the churchyard lie the bodies of those who died of that plague.

Also destroyed in the bombing was the Wool Exchange, which was erected in 1874 between Masons Avenue and White Horse Yard. A new Exchange has since been built in Commercial Street.

At the northern end of Coleman Street stands the

47

Armourers Hall. The armourers before the seventeenth century were one of the busiest of the City's companies. In the Hall can be seen a fine collection of armour and paintings of the sixteenth and seventeenth centuries. The hall of the Armourers Company has occupied the site for the last 500 years. The present building was erected in 1840, and needed considerable restoration after the bombing of the City.

COLLEGE HILL EC4 (Cannon Street) E4

The hill received its name in the fifteenth century when a college, founded by Richard Whittington, Lord Mayor of London, was built at the side of St Michael's church and called the college of St Spirit and St Mary; it stood next to the church until 1808 when it was demolished and moved to Highgate.

The Mercers Company built a school on the site but that also was removed, in 1894. Before the building of the college the hill was known as Paternosterstret, after the church of St Michael Paternoster. In the early fourteenth century the area was inhabited by French vintners who came from the town of La Riole near Bordeaux; the hill then became known as La Riole in honour of them, and the name of their town was added to the name of the church which became known as St Michael Paternoster Riole, which over the centuries has been corrupted to Royal. The church, which dates back to the thirteenth century, was destroyed in the Great Fire of 1666 and rebuilt by Wren in 1686. Richard Whittington was buried in the church in 1423, but his monument and grave were lost in the great fire. The church was badly bombed in the last war but has recently been completely restored. A tablet inside marks the site of Richard Whittington's burial place. Whittington lived in College Hill in the fifteenth century, and another tablet, on a wall near the church, marks the site of his house.

COLLEGE STREET EC4 (College Hill) E4

The street, like the hill, takes its name from the college founded by Richard Whittington. In the thirteenth century, before the College was built, the street was known as Le Arche, because at the eastern end the street became a little arched bridge, spanning the River Walbrook. In College Street stands the Hall of the Inn Holders, built in 1886. The hall was damaged by bombs in 1941, but has been rebuilt.

COOPERS ROW EC3 (Crutched Friars) H4

The street was named Coopers Row in the nineteenth century because of the large number of wine warehouses and coopers, or barrel-makers, working there.

Prior to that the street had been known as Woodroffe Lane in honour of the rich City family of that name living there. David Woodroffe was sheriff of London in 1554. A small painting on the wall of Talbot House, one of the last remaining houses in Coopers Row, shows a cluster of woodroffe, or wild flowers, growing in Woodroffe Lane, which flowers gave their name both to the family and to the street. The bombing of Coopers Row in 1941 destroyed many of the wine warehouses, and in so doing revealed one of the finest stretches of the Roman wall surrounding the City. It is 110 ft long and can be seen by entering the office block called Midland House. Another section of wall can be seen at the southern end of Coopers Row, next to Tower Hill station, and this section contains a replica of the Classicianus memorial. A piece of memorial stone found in 1935 matched a piece that had been discovered in 1852, and when the two were put together the Roman Latin inscription read:

In memory of Caius Julius Alpinus Classicianus of the Fabian tribe, procurator of the province of Britain, from Julia Pacata, daughter of Julius Indus, his sorrowing wife. AD 61.

This memorial can now be seen standing just inside the main entrance to the British Museum.

COPTHALL AVENUE EC2 (London Wall) F2

The avenue, built in 1890, takes its name from a large medieval house with a crested roof which was called Copped Hall, the word copped coming from the German *kopf*, in this instance describing the particularly sharp gable or roof of the house.

CORBET COURT EC3 (Gracechurch Street) F3

Named in memory of a family named Corbet whose house stood on this site in the seventeenth century, behind the church of St Peter, Cornhill. Miles Corbet was one of the men who plotted the execution of Charles I.

CORNHILL EC3 (The Bank) F3

The city's corn market stood in this street centuries ago on the side of one of the town's two hills, hence Cornhill. It is of great interest, however, to note that a gentleman named Edward Hupcornehill, a burgess of London in 1115, lived in the street. Cornhill, in medieval times, was one of the City's main streets. In the middle of the street stood a round house, or prison, called the Tun in Cornhill, built in 1282, which was a famous landmark for two centuries before being converted into a water conduit. The site today is marked by an old water pump standing near Royal Exchange Avenue. In 1582 a water conduit, the first to supply houses with water from the Thames through lead-covered pipes, was erected by Peter Morris, a Dutchman. The conduit, called the Standard, became very famous, and was eventually used as a point of measurement.

John Stow, the most famous of London historians, was born in Cornhill in the early sixteenth century. A tablet on number 41 Cornhill marks the site of the house in which Thomas Gray, the poet, was born in 1716. In the early eighteenth century, at the junction of Cornhill and Lombard Street, stood the bookshop of Thomas Guy who founded Guy's Hospital in 1721.

In modern Cornhill stand three buildings of interest, the Royal Exchange (see Royal Exchange), St Michael's church (see St Michaels Alley), and St Peter's church (see St Peters Alley).

COUSIN LANE EC4 (Upper Thames Street) E4

William Cosin was Sheriff of London in 1306, and the lane is named in memory of the Cosin family, whose house stood here in the fourteenth century.

COWPER'S COURT EC3 (Cornhill) F3

Cowper's Court was originally named Cooper's Court after Sir William Cooper, whose large town house occupied this site. Large vaults found during excavations for the rebuilding of an office block near Cowper's Court are believed to have belonged to the house. In the courtway stood a famous seventeenth-century coffee house called the Jerusalem, a popular rendezvous for City merchants. It was demolished to make way for another office block.

CRANE COURT EC4 (Fleet Street) A3

Named after a fourteenth-century brewhouse called the Crane and Three Hoops which stood on the site.

At the far end of Crane Court is the hall of the Royal Scottish Corporation (see Fetter Lane), which was bought from the Royal Society in 1782. The Royal Society, which was formed to discuss scientific matters, moved into the court in 1710. Their president at that time was Isaac Newton.

In the early days of newspapers when each one printed required a government stamp, Crane Court was notorious for the number of unstamped papers printed there. The papers were very often dispatched through a shute into the adjacent Fleur-de-Lys Court to evade the watchful eye of the government inspectors.

CREECHURCH LANE EC3 (Leadenhall Street) G3

So named because in the twelfth century the lane was a passageway leading to the priory of Holy Trinity, Christchurch, and *cree* was a common shortening of Christ. In the twelfth century the passage was called Cree Lane. The priory was built in 1108 at the request of Matilda, Queen of Henry I, and it occupied the whole of the area between Leadenhall Street, Creechurch Lane, and Dukes Place. London's first and longest-serving Lord Mayor, Henry Fitz Ailwyne, was buried in the church of the priory in 1212; he governed the City for twenty-four consecutive years. Henry VIII, at the dissolution of the monasteries, gave the priory to Sir Thomas Audley, who demolished it and in its place built a huge mansion. Through the marriage of his daughter the mansion passed into the hands of the Duke of Norfolk, whose son eventually sold it to the City of London for a sizeable sum. He used this money to build the stately home at Audley End. Long before the dissolution, in the late thirteenth century, a church was built in the grounds of the priory, and this church, St Katherine Cree, still stands on the corner of Leadenhall Street. It was one of the eight churches to survive the Great Fire of London, and contains the effigy of Sir Nicholas Throgmorton, who gave his name to Throgmorton Street.

At number 18 Creechurch Lane can be seen the original sign of the Crown and Three Sugar Loaves, a tavern, and below it the original name plate of Davison Newman, a firm who took over the inn and used it for their tea-retailing business. From this shop came the tea that was shipped to Boston harbour, was thrown into the sea at the Boston Tea Party, sparking off the American War of Independence.

A plaque on the corner of Bury Street marks the site of a synagogue which stood here between 1657 and 1701.

CREED LANE EC4 (Ludgate Hill) C3

The Credo or Creed was chanted on this corner as the clergy

Page 53 (above) Petticoat Lane on a Sunday morning; (below) 'The Fat Boy of Gluttony', Cock Lane

Page 54 (*above*) Printing House Square and *The Times* office, 1870; (*below*) the new *Times* building, occupying the old Printing House Square

of St Paul's walked in procession round the cathedral (see Amen Court).

CRESCENT EC3 (Minories) H4

Named purely because of its shape, the Crescent was almost completely destroyed in the bombing of 1940. A large section of Roman wall can now be seen standing between the Crescent and Coopers Row.

CRIPPLEGATE STREET EC1 (Golden Lane) D1

When the Saxons conquered London in the fifth or sixth centuries AD, one of the first things they did was to strengthen the Roman wall. On its northern side they constructed a new gate, and from that gate to the bastions, which can still be seen to the west of Monkwell Square, they built a tunnel, or *crepul*, along which the sentries crept to take up their positions in the bastions. The gate was, therefore, called Crepul Gate and the whole ward is called Cripplegate Ward. A plaque on the side of Roman House, Wood Street, marks the exact position of the gate, which was demolished in 1760.

Standing alone in the bomb-devastated Cripplegate Ward is the church of St Giles Cripplegate, which was first built about 1090; one of the few to escape the Fire of 1666, it suffered badly in the bombing of 1940. The memorial to John Milton, the poet, who was buried here in 1674, was destroyed in that bombing. The parish register records the marriage of Oliver Cromwell to Elizabeth Bouchier on 22 August 1620. The church has recently been completely restored by Godfrey Allen.

CROSBY SQUARE EC3 (Bishopsgate) G3

The square was built in 1677 on the site of a section of Crosby Hall that had been demolished. Crosby Hall, built in 1466 by Sir John Crosby, grocer and alderman of the City of London in 1461, was at that time the tallest private residence in the City. People came from far and wide to admire it. Sir John did not enjoy his mansion for long, for he died in 1475 and is buried in the adjacent St Helen's church. Crosby Hall then passed into the hands of Richard of Gloucester who, whilst living there, plotted the deaths of his nephews, Edward V and Richard, Duke of York, the two princes murdered in the Tower in 1483. Shakespeare, who lodged in nearby St Helens Place, refers to Crosby Hall in his play *Richard III*.

Sir Thomas More leased the house and here wrote his book *Life of Richard III*. More later sold the house to his best friend, an Italian merchant named Bonsivi, but when More was executed in the Tower Bonsivi returned the mansion to More's son-in-law in order that More's daughter could return to the place she loved. Alderman Bond bought the mansion in 1566, paying £1,500 for it.

The next owner, Sir John Spencer, Lord Mayor of London, suffered the indignity of having his daughter carried away in a baker's cart. He had forbidden her to see the man she loved, the Earl of Northampton, who disguised himself as a baker, hid her in his cart, and, to add insult to injury, accepted a sixpenny tip from her father. In the early seventeenth century the house fell into disrepair and was used for a time as a prison; in 1672 it became a Presbyterian meeting house, in 1800 it was used as a warehouse, and finally, in 1909, it was dismantled and transported to Cheyne Walk, Chelsea, where it was re-erected as a residence for women graduates studying under the auspices of the British Federation of University Women. Crosby Hall stands there to this day on the site of a property originally owned by Sir Thomas More in the sixteenth century.

CROSS KEY COURT EC2 (London Wall) E2

An inn called the Cross Keys standing here in the sixteenth century gave its name to this court. Crossed keys, the sign of St Peter, were a common inn sign in olden days, but when

Henry VIII dissolved the monasteries and broke away from Rome many inns dutifully changed their signs from the Crossed Keys to the Kynge's Heade.

CROSSWALL EC3 (Crutched Friars) H4

Crosswall is so named because it crossed the line of the old Roman wall, the course of which can be seen in Coopers Row, where a section was unearthed after the bombing of 1940. The name of the street up to the early twentieth century was John Street, after King John.

CROWN AND HORSESHOE WHARF EC4 (Upper Thames Street) C4

The wharf is probably named after an inn of that name which was erected near by in the late eighteenth century. In the early part of that century the wharf went under the unsavoury title of Dunghill Lane, presumably because it was situated near Puddle Dock, the watering place for horses.

CROWN COURT EC2 (Cheapside) E3

In the early fourteenth century Edward III erected a stone tower next to the church of St Mary le Bow, in place of a wooden one that had collapsed whilst his wife, Queen Philippa, who was standing on it at the time, was watching the jousting in Cheapside. The Queen was uninjured. The tower was called the Crown Seld, or Sildam, and in 1410 Henry IV gave it to the Mercers Company, who turned it into a warehouse and shops.

Crown Court remembers the Seld, as did Sir Christopher Wren when, in rebuilding the church of St Mary le Bow, he built a square tower under the steeple.

CROWN GARDENS EC3 (Aldgate High Street) H3

A sixteenth-century inn called the Crown stood on this site, and parts of it were discovered in the construction of Aldgate station.

CROWN OFFICE ROW EC4 (Middle Temple Lane) A4

An office erected for the Clerk of the Crown in the eighteenth century gave its name to this part of the Temple. Charles Lamb was born in Crown Office Row in 1775.

CRUTCHED FRIARS EC3 (Jewry Street) G4

In 1298 Ralph Hosiar and William Sabernes founded a convent called the Crossed or Crouched Friars of the Holy Cross, just inside the City wall. At the dissolution of the monasteries Henry VIII's minister, Thomas Cromwell, gave the church to a local carpenter, who converted it into a workshop. The great Hall of the Friars was turned into one of the City's first glass factories. According to Stow the whole of the convent was destroyed by a terrible fire in 1575. A section of the Roman wall can be seen in the basement of the large office block which stands on the eastern side of Crutched Friars, at its junction with Jewry Street.

CULLUM STREET EC3 (Fenchurch Street) G4

The house of Sir Thomas Cullum which stood on this site was completely destroyed in the Great Fire of 1666, and the street was built in its place.

Sir Thomas was born in Suffolk in 1587. When he was a young boy he was sent to the City as an apprentice to John Rayney, a draper. The apprenticeship expired and young Cullum was taken into the firm as a partner, opening a new business in Gracechurch Street. The drapery business flourished and Thomas Cullum became a rich man, was made an alderman and became a member of the Drapers Company. He became sheriff of London in 1646, and a year later was committed to the Tower for his part in the Royalist uprising in the City. In 1656 Sir Thomas retired to Bury St Edmunds where he died in 1664. His wife, who had died in 1637 at the age of thirty-five, bore him five sons and six daughters. She was buried in the church of All Hallows, Lombard Street, which was demolished in 1938.

CUNARD PLACE EC3 (Leadenhall Street) G3

Named after the great Cunard Steamship Company, whose offices stand in Leadenhall Street, next to Cunard Place. Sir Samuel Cunard was born in Halifax, Nova Scotia, in 1787. When steam power was introduced into the shipping world Cunard went into partnership with George Burns and David MacIver to carry out the British government's idea of substituting steamships for the old sailing ships. He founded the first Atlantic steamship line, which earned him a knighthood in 1859. Sir Samuel Cunard died on 28 April 1865.

CURSITOR STREET EC4 (Chancery Lane) A2

On this site stood the office of the Cursitor, the clerk in the court of Chancery who dealt with and wrote out ordinary everyday writs. In this street John Scott, afterwards Lord Chancellor Eldon, lived with his wife, Bessie Surtees; this was their first home after their elopement from Newcastle.

CUTLER STREET E1 (Houndsditch) G3

The Cutlers Company, makers of knives and all types of cutlery, owned a large portion of this area in the seventeenth century, and here they erected houses for their workers. The Cutlers Hall in those days stood in Cloak Lane, Cannon Street. The houses of the cutlery workers were pulled down when most of the work moved to the Sheffield area.

DARKHOUSE LANE EC4 (Upper Thames Street) D4

In the seventeenth century a tavern called the Darkhouse stood in the lane. The lane was known at that time as Dark Lane, a favourite haunt for prostitutes seeking seamen clients.

DEANS COURT EC4 (St Paul's churchyard) C3

The Deanery stands on the western side of the court adjoining the old Chorister School, which was founded by Dean Church in 1874. A new choir school has recently been completed on the eastern side of the cathedral, incorporating the bombed church of St Augustine-with-St-Faith.

DEVONSHIRE SQUARE EC2 (Bishopsgate) G2
In the sixteenth century a large house which stood on this site was owned by a city clerk and goldsmith named Jasper Fisher. Fisher was always in debt, and as the house he lived in was a further drain on his resources he was forced to sell it at a figure much lower than he had paid; he became a laughing stock among his friends, and the house was nicknamed Fisher's Folly. In 1620 the house came into the hands of the Earl of Devonshire, and was renamed Devonshire House. Charles II and the royal family were entertained there in 1660.

Devonshire House, like many old London mansions, fell into disrepair and was demolished, the square being built on its site. Devonshire Row was the old entrance to Devonshire House.

DISTAFF LANE EC4 (Cannon Street) D4
In this lane distaffs were made and sold to the weavers of the City. The distaff was the long stick that held the bunch of flax or wool used for spinning.

DORSET RISE EC4 (Tudor Street) B3
A huge mansion built in the twelfth century and owned by the bishops of Salisbury occupied the whole of this site, with gardens running down to the Thames. In the early seventeenth century James I gave the mansion to Richard, Earl of Dorset, the house then being renamed Dorset House. It became a sanctuary, free from the jurisdiction of the City, and no man could be arrested within its walls. It was completely destroyed in the Great Fire of London, 1666.

DOVE COURT EC2 (Old Jewry) E3
Pigeons and doves were bred on this part of the old poultry market, hence the name.

DOWGATE HILL EC4 (Cannon Street) E4

The River Walbrook, which was the City's main water supply in ancient times, flowed down this hill, through a water gate into the Thames. The name Dowgate or Downgate is thought to be derived from the force with which the river flowed down the hill to the gate. Alternatively the Celtic word *dwr*, meaning water, might have given its name to the gate, which certainly existed in Roman times and is considered to have been one of the earliest gates in the City.

Three of the City's livery companies' halls stand on the western side of Dowgate Hill. At number 10 stands the hall of the Dyers Company. The company, which was incorporated in 1472, has worked for centuries in close co-operation with the Weavers and Merchant Taylors of the City. The Dyers, like the Vintners, are privileged to keep swans on the Thames; they mark their birds with four bars and a nick on the bill. At number 8 is the Skinners Hall, which has occupied this site since the early thirteenth century; the present building, which was fortunate in escaping the bombing, was rebuilt after the Great Fire. At number 4 is the Hall of the Tallow Chandlers, or makers of tallow candles. The Hall, rebuilt by Sir Christopher Wren in 1672, was rebuilt again in 1871.

Sir Francis Drake lived in Dowgate Hill in a house called the Erber, a fourteenth-century mansion that had also accommodated Warwick the 'kingmaker', in the fifteenth century.

On the eastern side of Dowgate Hill stood the church of St Mary Bothaw, or Boat House, so named because it stood near the shipyards of the Thames, and almost opposite stood the church of St John the Baptist. Unfortunately both were destroyed in the Great Fire of 1666, and only the churchyards survived. The churchyards, too, disappeared with the building of Cannon Street station. Opposite College Street on the wall of the arches of the station which occupy the whole of the eastern side of Dowgate Hill can be seen some old parish boundary markers: 'St M B 1867' and 'St M R

61

1864'. These are the boundary markers of St Mary Bothaw and St Michael Paternoster Royal respectively. The church of St Michael Paternoster Royal has been recently restored in College Street.

DRAPERS GARDENS EC2 (Throgmorton Avenue) F3
The gardens of the Drapers Company exist now in name only, having long been built upon. The garden was one of the City's beauty spots, taking up the complete area behind the hall.

DUCKSFOOT LANE EC4 (Upper Thames Street) E4
A pathway leading from the Duke of Suffolk's house to the River Thames was called Dukes Foot Lane, which, over the years, has been corrupted to Ducksfoot Lane. The house, which was known as the Manor of the Rose, was built in the fourteenth century by Sir John Pountney, Lord Mayor of London. The house was later acquired by the Dukes of Suffolk and passed through many hands until, in 1561, part of it was purchased for the Merchant Taylors company, who built one of their schools there. The school stood on this site until 1873 when it was removed to the Charterhouse, near Smithfield.

DUKES PLACE EC3 (Aldgate) H3
The house of Thomas Howard, Duke of Norfolk, stood on this site. The house, which the Duke had acquired from Sir Thomas Audley, was built on the site of the priory of Holy Trinity (see Creechurch Lane). On the western side of Dukes Place can be seen the eighteenth-century John Cass school, one of London's charity schools, founded originally to help educate the City's poor children. The statues of charity children can still be seen above the doorways of the school. Sir John Cass, social benefactor, was alderman of the Portsoken ward, became Sheriff of London in 1711, and was knighted in the following year.

On the same side of the street stands the bombed shell of the Great Synagogue which was first built in 1789 for German and Polish Jews. The synagogue now continues in Addler Street, Commercial Road.

DUNSTER COURT EC3 (Mincing Lane) G4

Before this area was destroyed by German bombs a little courtway called Dunster Court stood at the northern end of Mincing Lane, next to the Clothworkers Hall. Dunster is a corruption of St Dunstan, the church of that name which stood a little to the south of Mincing Lane. Dunster Court is now the name given to a huge office block which was built on the bombed site. The office block includes the hall of the Clothworkers Company, the twelfth of the twelve great livery companies and particularly famous for the charitable funds it administers all over Britain. The company dates back to 1482 and its Master in 1677 was Sir Samuel Pepys, the diarist.

DYERS BUILDINGS EC1 (Holborn) A2

Here stood almshouses belonging to the Dyers Company. William Roscoe lived in Dyers Buildings in 1824 when his ten volumes on the works of Alexander Pope, were published.

EASTCHEAP EC1 (Gracechurch Street) F4

Eastcheap was so called to distinguish it from the West Cheap market (now Cheapside). It was one of the main marketplaces of Roman London, and continued to flourish as a marketplace through the Anglo-Saxon period. In medieval times it was the City's main meat market, butchers' stalls lining both sides of the street. The market was eventually removed to the newly built Leadenhall market in the early eighteenth century. One of London's most celebrated taverns, the Boars Head, stood at the western end of Eastcheap, though the actual site was swept away when King

William Street was built as an approach road to London Bridge.

In the eighteenth century the Boars Head became the meeting place of the Falstaff Club, each member assuming the name of a Shakesperian character. A boar's head carved in relief on stone and dated 1668 was discovered in 1811, and can be seen in the Guildhall museum. A tavern called the Falstaff now stands at the western end of Eastcheap.

On the corner of Rood Lane and Eastcheap stands the church of St Margaret Pattens, which is mentioned as early as the fourteenth century. It was unfortunately destroyed in the Fire of 1666, but was rebuilt by Wren in 1684. The church is thought to derive its name from pattenmakers living near by, although many historians mention the fact that a family named Paten lived here in the fourteenth century.

EAST HARDING STREET EC4 (Great New Street) B3
In 1513 the whole of this area was left in the will of widow Agnes Harding to the Goldsmiths Company, who built houses on the site; many of these bore the old arms of the Company, until the bombing and reconstruction.

EAST PASSAGE EC1 (Cloth Street) D1
East Passage follows the line of the eastern boundary of the precinct of the ancient Bartholomew Priory which originally occuped this site. The priory was founded by Rahere, the court jester of Henry I, in 1123.

EAST PAULS WHARF EC4 (Upper Thames Street) C4
The wharf stands east of the old Pauls Wharf which was leased to the dean of St Paul's cathedral in the fifteenth century.

ELDON STREET EC2 (Blomfield Street) F2
John Scott was a young barrister who eloped from New-

castle with his wife-to-be, Bessie Surtees. He became a famous figure in the Middle Temple in the 1770s; he was created Lord Chancellor in 1801 and in 1821 was made Earl of Eldon. At one time he held the post of Governor of Charterhouse and was also a Trustee of the British Museum. The street is named in his honour.

ELM COURT EC4 (Old Bailey) C3
In the fourteenth century a tavern called Le Elme stood in Fleet Street. It was the favourite tavern of William Walworth, the slayer of Wat Tyler—the leader of the Peasants' Revolt in 1381. The court is named after the tavern.

ESSEX COURT EC4 (Middle Temple) A3
Essex Court stands on the site of the eastern wing of the huge Essex House, which once occupied the whole of the area south of modern Aldwych. The house was built in the early fourteenth century by Walter de Stapledon, who was Bishop of Exeter and Lord Treasurer of England. It brought bad luck and a violent end to a succession of owners. In 1326 it was sacked by a mob who dragged the bishop to the Standard in Cheapside and beheaded him. The next owner, Thomas Howard, Duke of Norfolk, was beheaded in 1572 for supporting the cause of Mary Queen of Scots in her efforts to obtain the throne of England. Robert Dudley, Earl of Leicester, the owner of Essex House, was alleged to have poisoned his guest, Sir Nicholas Throgmorton, the famous City merchant. Next came Robert Devereux, Earl of Essex, the acknowledged favourite of Queen Elizabeth I; he was taken from the house in 1601 and beheaded on Tower Green for his part in an uprising.

Eventually the huge house was divided into two parts. The eastern portion was purchased by the Middle Temple for its own expansion and demolished; on its site was erected New Court, Garden Court, and Essex Court. On the site of the other portion stand modern streets—Norfolk Street,

Howard Street, Essex Street, and Devereux Court—all perpetuating the names of various owners of Essex House. These streets lie outside the City boundary.

EXCHANGE BUILDINGS EI (Cutler Street) G3
In the nineteenth century a building called the Clothes Exchange stood opposite this courtway.

FALCON COURT EC4 (Fleet Street) A3
A sixteenth-century tavern called the Falcon stood in Fleet Street near this court. In the early seventeenth century Falcon Court was a passageway leading directly to the Temple church.

FALCON SQUARE EC1 (London Wall) D2
Falcon Square remains in name only at the south-west corner of London Wall, for the square was obliterated when the first bombs fell on the City in August 1940. Falcon Street and Falcon Avenue also disappeared. All these streets took their names from one of the City's most famous coaching inns, the Castle and Falcon, which stood on the eastern side of Aldersgate Street, opposite St Botolph's church. The inn was formerly the house of John Day, an Elizabethan printer and publisher, who used as his crest a falcon sitting on a castle. It was eventually demolished to make way for new office buildings on that side of Aldersgate Street.

FAN COURT EC4 (Miles Lane) F4
In the fourteenth century when fresh meat was bought from the butchers' stalls in Eastcheap and Pudding Lane the butchers had a scalding house in Pudding Lane, which later became known as Fanners Hall. *Fanning* was the butchers' way of keeping the meat cool, hence the name.

FARRINGDON STREET EC4 (Ludgate Circus) B3
Alderman William Farendon was a City merchant of the

Goldsmiths Company, who purchased this ward in 1279 and became alderman of it in 1281. Farringdon Street was named in his honour.

Beneath modern Farringdon Street runs the old River Fleet, which has long since been converted into a sewer. Farringdon Street was built in 1738 upon arches so as to lift it several feet above the river, and upon its completion the old Stocks market, which had been used to accommodate the Lord Mayor's Mansion House, occupied the whole of the middle of the street. The market, known as the Fleet market, flourished until 1829 when increasing traffic made it necessary to widen the road.

On the eastern side of the street near Ludgate Circus stands the Memorial Hall, a sombre-looking building erected in 1874 in honour of more than 2,000 clergymen of the Church of England who refused in 1662 to abide by the Act of Uniformity and were expelled from their Church.

On the wall of the Memorial Hall is a plaque commemorating the notorious Fleet Prison, demolished in 1846. The prison which was one of the most dreaded in London, was erected on the eastern bank of the Fleet in the twelfth century, but the building was completely destroyed in the Great Fire of 1666. It was later rebuilt and in the seventeenth century was converted into a prison for debtors; farcical situations would arise inside—for instance clergymen, imprisoned for debt, would perform illegal marriages there. Customers were touted for by the warders, who then received their share of the fee from the clergy. Lovers, elopers, and gin-sodden harlots with their drunken men friends flocked to the prison to be united in a 'Fleet marriage', as these unions were then called. After the wedding the couples would make their way to the Hoop and Grapes tavern opposite the prison; it can still be seen, snuggled between modern office buildings. Before the war, Nash's, as the Hoop and Grapes was more often called, held a licence to open in the early hours of the morning to cater for the porters of Smith-

67

field market. This early licence and the good food sold there made the pub one of the most famous in London; taxi-drivers on night shift drove there for their breakfast and often recommended the pub to late-night revellers who wished to carry on drinking. The pub no longer holds the early-morning licence but is still popular with City workers for its fine food. Although the outside of the Hoop and Grapes has been modernised, the inside is over 300 years old, and is full of character.

FENCHURCH STREET EC3 (Gracechurch Street) F4

The street took its name from a church called St Gabriel Fenchurch which stood in the centre of the road between Rood Lane and Mincing Lane. The word *fen* was derived from the Latin *fenum*, meaning hay, as this was sold at the western end of the street in the grass market (Gracechurch Street). Another theory is that a stream called the Lang-bourn flowed along the street, causing the ground to be fenny or moorish, but no trace of it has ever been found—although the Ward has for centuries been known as Langbourn.

The church of St Gabriel was completely destroyed in the Great Fire of London and was not rebuilt. Before the bomb-ing of the City a portion of the old graveyard could still be seen in Fen Court. The graveyard has now been completely paved over, but a tablet on the eastern side of the court marks its site.

On the western corner of Lime Street stood a church called St Dionis Backchurch, first built in the thirteenth century but destroyed in the Fire of 1666. Sir Christopher Wren rebuilt it, but it was eventually demolished in 1878 to make way for new office buildings. St Dionis was called *Backchurch* because it stood at the side of the street, whereas St Gabriel, in the centre of the roadway, was called *Fore-church*.

On the northern side of Fenchurch Street, near Billiter Street, stood the Hall of the Ironmongers Company, which had occupied the same site since 1457. The Hall was fortunate in escaping the flames of the Great Fire, but was destroyed 250 years later when, in 1917, a German bomb scored a direct hit on it. The Ironmongers Company rebuilt its hall in Aldersgate Street in 1925.

On the corner of Mark Lane stood the famous Kings Head tavern; here Princess Elizabeth ate pork and peas to celebrate her release in 1554 from the Tower of London, after first having given thanks at the nearby church of All Hallows Staining, the tower of which can still be seen in Star Alley.

On the southern side of the street, near the entrance to Fenchurch Street railway station, stood the church of St Catherine Coleman, which escaped the Great Fire but was allowed to fall into disrepair and eventually had to be demolished in the 1920s. A large office block called Haddon House was erected on its site. The churchyard of St Catherine Coleman can still be seen with its original railings and its old church notice board, faded but is still legible.

A little farther to the east, on the corner of Lloyds Avenue, stands the building of Lloyd's, publishers of the *Register of Shipping*. The next alleyway eastwards is Northumberland Alley, which marks the site of Northumberland House, the town house of the Earls of Northumberland, destroyed in the Great Fire.

FETTER LANE EC4 (Fleet Street) A3
In the sixteenth century the lane was called Fewtors Lane, derived from the Norman French word *fewtor*, meaning an idle person. The lane had a reputation as the meeting place of the City's down-and-outs and loafers who would idle away their time there.

John Dryden, the poet, lived in Fetter Lane in the seventeenth century. His house was pulled down in 1887.

A Moravian chapel was built in the seventeenth century, and Thomas Bradbury, John and Charles Wesley, and George Whitefield all preached in it. The chapel was destroyed in the bombing of the City. Midway along Fetter Lane, near the Three Tuns public house, stands the hall of the Scottish Corporation, which was formed in the reign of James I to help Scots, resident in London, who were in distress; for when James VI of Scotland became James I of England many Scots followed him to London.

At the Fleet Street end of Fetter Lane, on the western side, stands Cliffords Inn, which was formerly the house of Robert de Clifford, a gift from his reigning monarch, Edward II, in the early fourteenth century. In 1345 the house was given to students of the law and became one of the first Inns of Court. The Inn became famous in 1666 after the Great Fire of London, for here sat Sir Matthew Hall and seventeen other judges to adjudicate the claims of all who had lost property in that fire; their findings, some forty volumes in all, are preserved in the British Museum. Cliffords Inn did not escape the bombing of the Second World War, but the name is retained in the office block that was built in its place. The old gatehouse of the original Inn survived the bombing and can still be seen in the gardens of the office buildings.

FINCH LANE EC3 (Cornhill) F3

Robert Finke, a thirteenth-century city merchant, was a benefactor to the church of St Benet, his name being added to that of the church, which then became St Benet Fink. The church stood on the southern side of Threadneedle Street, and although it was destroyed in the Great Fire it was rebuilt by Wren in 1673. In 1844 the church was pulled down to make way for the improvement of the Royal Exchange, and Royal Exchange buildings now occupies the site.

FINSBURY CIRCUS EC2 (Moorgate) F2

The Circus, a self-explanatory name, was constructed in the early nineteenth century when the old Bethlehem, or Bedlam, hospital was removed from London Wall and the whole

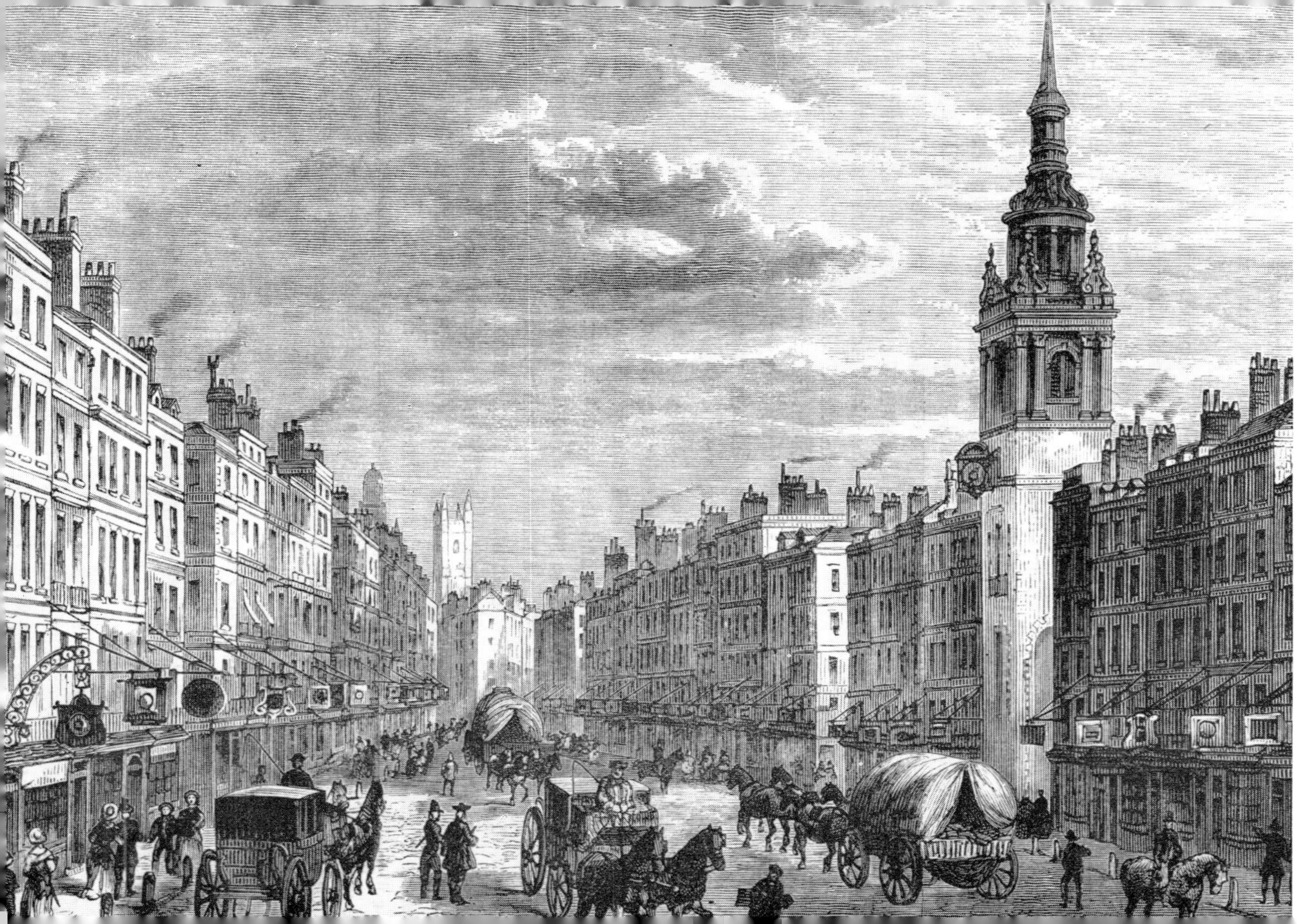

Page 71 Bow Church and Cheapside in 1750

Page 72 (*above*) Bow Church and Cheapside, 1969; (*below*) a section of the new London Bridge being lowered into place (1969?). The old bridge is being sent to the USA

area redesigned. On the northern side there stood until 1912 the School of Oriental Studies, its site now occupied by one of the many large office blocks which surround the oval-shaped gardens. Finsbury derives its name from ancient days when most of the area to the north of the city was marshland, and this particular part was known as Fernsbury, presumably because of the quantities of ferns growing on the marshy land. The open land was used by women to dry their washing, and also by the City's trained bands, who found it ideal for archery practice. The land was also used as a burial ground for the thousands of victims of the plague of 1665; the burial ground, known as Bone Fields, was later turned into an official cemetery and called Bunhill Fields. In it lies John Wesley, the nonconformist preacher, whose chapel still stands in City Road opposite the cemetery. Also buried there are John Bunyan (1688), the author of *Pilgrim's Progress*, and Daniel Defore (1731), who wrote *Robinson Crusoe*. In the early eighteenth century the marshy land was drained and made into gardens, and in 1789 Finsbury Square, known then as Finsbury Pavement, was laid out by George Dance. It was the first pathway to be paved in the marshy area. Finsbury Circus was built soon afterwards. The area became a fashionable quarter for doctors, but they later vacated the City for the newly built Wimpole and Harley Streets situated a few miles west. John Keats the poet was born in Finsbury Pavement in 1795. Of the places mentioned only Finsbury Circus lies inside the City boundary.

FISH STREET HILL EC3 (Eastcheap) F4

Fish Street was formerly known as New Fish Street to distinguish it from Old Fish Street which was demolished in 1870 to make way for the new Queen Victoria Street.

A new London Bridge was constructed in 1831, but the old London Bridge stood approximately 180 ft to the east in a direct line with Fish Street Hill. Before the Great Fire of 1666 a traveller from Southwark, having crossed London

Bridge, would pass the western wall of St Magnus the Martyr and continue up Fish Street Hill, or New Fish Street, as it was then called. On the eastern side, halfway up the hill, he would have passed the church of St Margaret, which was to be consumed in the flames and not rebuilt. A little farther along the same side was a hostelry called the Black Bell, which in the fourteenth century had been the home of the Black Prince, the son of Edward III; and at the end of the hill, on the eastern corner of Eastcheap, stood another church called St Leonard's; but both the inn and the church were destroyed in the Great Fire, which started just round the corner in Pudding Lane (2 September 1666).

FISHMONGERS HALL STREET EC4 (Upper Thames Street) F5

The hall of the Fishmongers Company towers above this narrow little street, which runs to the River Thames at the western side of the bridge. The Fishmongers Company was formed in the early thirteenth century to safeguard and inspect the fishmarket of the City. In the reign of James I the Fishmongers were made responsible for the inspection of the fish at nearby Billingsgate Market; they still hold this responsibility but can only seize a consignment of fish with the authority of a City magistrate. One of the most famous members of the Fishmongers Company was William Walworth who slew Wat Tyler, the leader of the Peasants' Revolt, at Smithfield in 1381. A statue of Walworth is the proud possession of the Company.

Another famous member was Thomas Dogget, who in 1716 left in his will a sum of money for the purpose of purchasing an orange coat and silver Hanoverian badge to be contended for by six young watermen annually on the 1 August. That race, known as Dogget's Coat and Badge race, still takes place between London Bridge and the Old Swan at Chelsea. The old Fishmongers Hall was destroyed in the Great Fire of 1666 but it was rebuilt soon afterwards.

74

The Hall was completely rebuilt again in 1831–4 from a design by H. Roberts. Today the Fishmongers Company, apart from inspecting the fish at Billingsgate, also tries to prevent the pollution of England's rivers and the spread of diseases, particularly typhoid.

FLEET LANE EC4 (Farringdon Street) B3
In former times the lane ran from the Old Bailey to the Fleet River, from which it takes its name. A stone bridge at the end of Fleet Lane enabled pedestrians to cross to the other bank.

FLEET RIVER
The course of the old River Fleet, or *Fleot* as it was known in Anglo-Saxon, can be traced on a modern map of London by the street names under which it flows. Its source lay in the hills of Hampstead, near the Vale of Health, and it flowed down Willow Road to South End Green, where it is remembered in Fleet Road. From here it bore an easterly line across Lismore Circus and then turned south to the east of Weedington Road and crossed Prince of Wales Road, near Kentish Town station, to Hawley Road. Here the river gained strength by a merger with an eastern tributary that flowed from the hills of Highgate, and then ran southwards between Royal College Street and St Pancras Way, down Pancras Road to Battle Bridge at the rear of Kings Cross station. From here the Fleet ran between Grays Inn Road and Kings Cross Road to the junction of Farringdon Road and Clerks Well, or Clerkenwell as it is now known. Then the river ran due south, following the line of Farringdon Street and New Bridge Street to enter the Thames near Blackfriars Bridge.

Five bridges crossed the river, the most southerly being the Bridewell bridge connecting the old Palace of Bridewell with Blackfriars priory. That stretch of river is now New Bridge Street. At Ludgate Circus stood the largest of the bridges, which connected the Fleet Bridge Road, now known as Fleet Street, to the old Lud Gate and Ludgate Hill. Middle Bridge spanned the Fleet where Fleet Lane joins Farringdon Street, and this bridge was used by prisoners going to the Fleet Prison (now the Memorial Hall), which stood on the corner of Fleet Lane. The large Holborn bridge at the point where Snow Hill joins Farringdon Street enabled pedestrians travelling from New Gate down Snow Hill to proceed up Holborn Hill. Holborn Viaduct was built in 1869 to connect these hills. The last bridge crossed the river at modern Cowcross Street, which lies outside the City boundary; the Cow Bridge was used by cattle going to Smithfield market.

The river became polluted as early as the thirteenth century and the southern stretch was later called the Fleet Ditch. In 1735 an Act of Parliament was passed to cover it over between Fleet Bridge and Holborn Bridge, and after this was done the Fleet market was erected on the site in 1737. By 1855 the whole of the river was covered in and utilised as the main sewer, into which all the little sewers of Hampstead, Kentish Town, Kings Cross, and Clerkenwell run. This main sewer carries the refuse of north London and the City into the Thames.

FLEET STREET EC4 (Temple Bar to Ludgate Circus) A3

The Fleet river (see page 75) is of course perpetuated in the name of the street. In the thirteenth century the Fleet Bridge connected Ludgate Hill to Fleet Street. Along the southern side of the street stood three great buildings: Bridewell Palace was on the corner of Fleet Street and the river (now New Bridge Street), a little farther west stood the great Whitefriars priory, and farther west the Temple, home of the Knights Templars. Over the preceding centuries many great houses were built and eventually demolished.

Between the sixteenth and eighteenth centuries Fleet Street became fashionable with actors, authors, and poets, who frequented its many taverns and coffee houses. The ghosts of Ben Jonson, Dean Swift, Alexander Pope, Oliver Goldsmith, Dr Johnson, and James Boswell still haunt the little courtways of Fleet Street, which has been for the last 100 years the home of British journalism. At the western end today stands the Griffin, which was erected in 1878 on the site of the famous Temple Bar, a gateway built by Wren in 1672, and was eventually removed because it became a traffic hazard; it had a certain fame, or notoriety, for as late as the 1770s the heads of executed persons were exhibited on it for all the City to see. It marked the boundary between the City and Westminster and now forms an entrance to Theobalds Park, Cheshunt.

At number 1 Fleet Street stands Childs Bank, the oldest private bank in England. It was founded in 1560 and built on the site of the old Marigold tavern, the bank adopting the inn sign and displaying a marigold on all its cheques. Royalty patronised Childs—Charles II, James II, Oliver Cromwell, William and Mary all banked here. A plaque on the bank marks the site of the famous old Devil tavern where Ben Jonson presided over the celebrated Apollo Club, whose membership later included Samuel Pepys, Pope, Goldsmith, Johnson, and Boswell. The tavern was demolished in 1788 to make way for the extension of Child's Bank. On the same side are the gates to the Middle Temple, which were built by Wren in 1684. Opposite Chancery Lane stands one of the oldest buildings in London, dating from 1611; it is called Prince Henry's Room, and was the old council room of the Duke of Cornwall, Prince Henry, the son of James I. The old Cock tavern on the same side was built in 1887, its more famous predecessor having stood almost opposite on the other side of the street.

On the northern side stands the church of St Dunstan-in-the-West, which was completely rebuilt in 1831; the original church dated back to the early thirteenth century. William Tyndale, translator of the New Testament, was vicar of St Dunstan's in the period 1528–36. Its great clock towers above

77

the pavement and is said to be the first to have minute divisions; the clubbed giants who strike the hour are firm favourites with Fleet Street workers. On the eastern side of the church, above the vestry door, is a full-size statue of Queen Elizabeth I, which formerly stood above the old Lud Gate, and was transferred to its present position when the gate was demolished in 1760.

Opposite the church is another famous bank, which displays as its sign a golden bottle. Hoare's bank was founded *c* 1673 by James Hoare, whose favourite tavern was the Golden Bottle in Cheapside, and he adopted the inn sign for his bank. A plaque at the side of the bank marks the site of the Old Mitre tavern, another Fleet Street drinking house, made famous by Dr Johnson. The tavern was demolished in 1829 when Hoare's bank was enlarged. Many of the old taverns still stand today: on the southern side are The Cock, The Falstaff, The Old Bell and the Punch Tavern. On the northern side is the celebrated Cheshire Cheese, and on the corner of Fetter Lane is Peele's, a tavern that has occupied the same site for over 400 years; the Duke of Wellington, Lord Macaulay, Charles Dickens, and Samuel Johnson all frequented it.

At the eastern end of the street stand the great offices of the national daily newspapers, the *Daily Telegraph* and the *Daily Express*. Opposite the *Daily Express* is the office of Reuters, the famous world news organisation.

Fleet Street also has another full-size statue of a queen: above the doorway of number 143 stands the statue of Mary Queen of Scots. Inside the doorway on the right-hand wall is a poem dedicated to Mary, 'Adieux de Marie Stuart à la France', by the French poet Beranger. The statue and the poem belonged to a Scottish laird, Sir John Tollemache Sinclair, a former owner of the property. The poem is translated into English on the opposite wall. At the extreme eastern end of Fleet Street, in Ludgate Circus, is a tablet on the wall of a bank remembering Edgar Wallace, the Fleet Street journalist

78

turned author who died in Hollywood in 1932. Wren's church of St Bride's stands on the southern side of Fleet Street at the Ludgate Circus end (see St Brides Avenue).

FLEUR-DE-LYS COURT EC4 (Fetter Lane) A3
The name of the court is taken from an old tavern called the Flower-de-Luce, the emblem of the kings of France. In the court in 1767 lived Mrs Elizabeth Brownrigge, a midwife of St Dunstan's workhouse, who beat her young apprentice Mary Mitchell until she died. Mrs Brownrigge was tried at the Old Bailey and found guilty; she was hung at Tyburn and her body was then taken to the Surgeons Hall for dissection.

FORE STREET EC2 (Wood Street) E2
The Old English word *fore* means that the street ran immediately before (outside) the wall. Fore Street, outside the City wall, was used by travellers entering the City either at Aldermanbury postern gate or the larger Cripplegate. The street suffered badly during the war and a tablet on the side of the modern block called Roman House marks the site where the first bomb fell on the City, at 12.15 am on 25 August 1940.

FOSTER LANE EC2 (Cheapside) D3
Named after the church of St Vedast, which stands on the eastern side of the street. Here is a good example of how, over the centuries, a name can be corrupted. In the thirteenth century the street was called St Vedast Lane, in the fourteenth century St Fasterslane, in the fifteenth century plain Fastourlane, and in the late sixteenth century Foster Lane. The church of St Vedast has occupied this site since the early thirteenth century. It was partially destroyed by the Great Fire and was rebuilt by Wren between 1695 and 1700. St Vedast was once bishop of Arras in France.

At the corner of Gresham Street stands the Hall of the Goldsmiths Company, which ranks fifth of the twelve great livery companies. The Goldsmiths Hall has occupied this site for the last 600 years, though the present Hall, restored after the bombing in World War II, dates from 1835. The Company, which was incorporated in 1327, is responsible for assaying and stamping all articles of gold and silver. It also has the privilege of testing the coins of the realm which are made in the Royal Mint. On the western side of the street once stood a church called St Leonard's; rebuilt in 1631, it was only to be destroyed in the Great Fire of 1666.

FOUNDERS COURT EC2 (Lothbury) E3
In the sixteenth century the Founders Hall stood on this site. It is believed that it was the *loathsome* noise made by the founders hammering iron and brass that gave rise to the name of Lothbury (page 128). The Founders Hall was removed in 1845 to St Swithins Lane.

FOUNTAIN COURT EC4 (Middle Temple Lane) A4
The fountain in the Middle Temple marks a retreat for lawyers and city clerks, and gave its name to the court.

FOWKES BUILDING EC3 (Great Tower Street) G5
John Fowke, a member of the Haberdashers Company, built a number of houses in what was then known as Tower Street, and these were granted to Christ's Hospital, which stood in Newgate Street. In 1652 Fowke became Lord Mayor of London, and he was knighted in the following year by Oliver Cromwell.

FOX AND KNOT COURT EC1 (Charterhouse Street) C1
A tavern called the Fox and Knot stood at the western end of Charterhouse Street in Chick Lane, which was a street once notorious for pickpockets and part of one of the City's worst slum areas. The tavern and the whole area were demolished when Smithfield market was laid out in the nineteenth century.

FREDERICKS PLACE EC2 (Old Jewry) E3

The mansion of Sir John Frederick, a member of the Grocers Company, stood on this site. Sir John was elected Lord Mayor of London in 1661, one of the 109 members of the Grocers Company to hold this office. In 1680 he was president of Christ's Hospital in Newgate Street, and he donated a large sum of money to be used for the rebuilding of its hall, which was destroyed in the Great Fire of 1666. Christ's Hospital stood in Newgate Street until 1902, when it was removed to make way for the General Post Office buildings. A plaque marks the site of the hospital.

FRENCH ORDINARY COURT EC3 (Crutched Friars) G4

In the seventeenth century the word 'ordinary' referred to the 'ordinary' or everyday meals sold by a small restaurant, and at the end of this little courtway, which now forms a rear entrance to Fenchurch Street station, stood one of these restaurants where an ordinary French meal could be obtained. The restaurant was razed to the ground in the Great Fire of 1666.

FRIAR STREET EC4 (Carter Lane) C3

The Blackfriars monastery which occupied the whole of this area was built by Dominican monks in 1276. The monastery was dissolved by Henry VIII in the sixteenth century, and the street is named in its memory (see Blackfriars Lane).

FRIDAY STREET EC4 (Queen Victoria Street) D4

The fishmongers of the City sold their fish in this street, the majority of their trade being done on a Friday; for at this time all England belonged to the Catholic faith and Friday was a meatless day.

Before the construction of Queen Victoria Street in 1871 and the destruction of this area in 1940–41 by German bombs, Friday Street ran between Old Fish Street and Cheapside. The church of St Matthew stood on the western side of the street near Cheapside, from the early thirteenth century until it was destroyed by the Great Fire of 1666. Wren rebuilt the church but it was pulled down in the late nineteenth century to make way for a new office building. Another church, St John the Evangelist, stood on the eastern side of the street at the junction of Watling Street, and towards the southern end stood a third church, St Margaret Moses; both these were burnt down in the Great Fire and not rebuilt.

FURNIVAL STREET EC4 (Holborn) A2
Though formerly called Castle Street the street was renamed in memory of Sir William Furnival who, in the year 1408, granted a house and some land situated on the opposite side of Holborn to students of law, and they converted the house into an Inn of Chancery. The Inn was completely rebuilt in 1818. Charles Dickens lived in the Inn in the 1830s and here he wrote *Pickwick Papers*. In 1850 the Inn was converted into Wood's Hotel, but that was demolished in 1897 and the huge red-brick building of the Prudential Assurance Company was erected on its site. A plaque just inside the main entrance of the building marks the site where Dickens lived.

GARLICK HILL EC4 (Upper Thames Street) D4
Garlic was sold at the foot of this hill near the riverside, and because of this the area acquired the name Garlick Hythe. In Garlick Hill, at its junction with Upper Thames Street, is the church of St James Garlickhythe, which was built in the twelfth century and rebuilt in 1606, only to be destroyed sixty years later in the Great Fire. Wren later rebuilt it at a cost of £5,357 12s 10d. The church suffered again in the bombing of London, but has since been completely restored. An interesting relic displayed inside, in a glass case, is the body of a man, almost completely preserved, which was discovered in 1839 by workmen closing up the old vaults.

On the western side of the street is the Beaver Hall, the fur-auction rooms of the Hudson's Bay Company. Opposite Beaver Hall can be seen the showrooms and workshops of the fur trade. Fur traders from many countries can be seen discussing business in the street on weekdays.

GILTSPUR STREET C2

Knights in their shining armour rode their horses through this street to the jousting grounds at the *Smoothfield* (since corrupted to Smithfield).

A plaque on the wall at the south-east corner of the street marks the site of the Giltspur Street Comptor, or house of correction, which was demolished in 1854. Almost opposite, beside St Sepulchre's church, stands the old church Watch House (a lookout for body snatchers), erected in 1791. It was bombed in 1941 but rebuilt in 1962. A bust of Charles Lamb, now on the Watch House, was transferred there from the bombed ruin of Wren's Christ Church in Newgate Street, in memory of Lamb's days as a pupil of Christ's Hospital, or the 'Bluecoat School', which once stood on the site now occupied by the GPO transport yard.

In the transport yard on the eastern side of Giltspur Street, where the GPO vans are garaged, is a large portion of the old Roman wall. Next to the GPO yard is St Bartholomew's hospital, founded in 1123 by Rahere, the court jester of Henry I. Rahere also founded the St Bartholomew priory, of which only the church remains, in Little Britain. The hospital was completely rebuilt in 1730–59 from a design by James Gibbs, though the old gatehouse was built a little earlier, in 1702. Since the hospital was founded soldiers wounded at the battles of Crecy (1346), Agincourt (1415), Blenheim (1704), Waterloo (1815), and the two world wars have been treated there .

Inside the hospital is the church of St Bartholomew the Less. Founded in 1123, it escaped the Great Fire of 1666 but, due to deterioration, had to be rebuilt in 1789 and again in

83

1823. Inigo Jones, the famous architect, was baptised there in 1573.

Opposite the hospital, on the corner of Cock Lane, can be seen the Golden Fat Boy statue, marking the spot where the Great Fire of London eventually petered out on Wednesday, 5 September 1666. The statue was rescued from the tavern called the Fortune of War which perished in the final flames. That corner of Cock Lane was known as Pie Corner.

GLASSHOUSE ALLEY EC4 (Bouverie Street) B3
On this site in the seventeenth century stood one of the City's glass factories.

GODLIMAN STREET EC4 (Queen Victoria Street) C4
In the sixteenth century the shoemakers of the area lived and worked mainly in Godalming in Surrey. The City shoemakers named their street Godalming Street in their honour, the name over the centuries, probably due to the nearness of St Paul's, being corrupted to Godliman. The Cordwainers Hall, which stood for centuries in Cannon Street, was blasted out of existence by German bombs, and has not been rebuilt. A plaque on the wall of the gardens at the eastern end of St Paul's cathedral marks the site of the old Shoemakers Hall.

GOLDEN FLEECE COURT EC3 (Minories) H4
A tavern called the Golden Fleece stood on this site. The Fleece was a common inn sign in the thirteenth and fourteenth centuries when fleece or wool was the country's major export and tax-raiser.

GOLDEN LANE EC1 (Beech Street) D1
In the thirteenth century a family named Goldyng lived here, and for centuries the street was known as Goldyng Lane.

On the eastern side of the lane stood the celebrated Fortune theatre, built in the year 1600 for the actor Edward Alleyn. It became one of the best known of all Elizabethan

84

theatres and Alleyn used the profits from it to found Alleyn's College at Dulwich. The original Fortune was built of wood and was completely destroyed by fire in 1621. A new theatre was erected, this time built of stone, but this, too, was partially destroyed in 1649 by Puritan soldiers. The theatre was finally demolished in 1661, but in 1678 a nursery school for child actors was erected near the site. Before bombs obliterated the whole of this area in 1940 a little alleyway connected Golden Lane with Whitecross Street, and it was called Playhouse Yard in memory of the old Fortune. A new thoroughfare has been cut through the blitzed buildings, and the City corporation has named it Fortune Street.

The Cripplegate Institute stands on the western side of the lane. The foundation stone of the institute was laid in 1894 by the Duke of York (later King George V) and the completed building, containing a theatre and library, is used specifically by students of drama and opera and secretarial subjects. A statue of John Milton, the poet, stands just inside the main entrance. In the late 1950s the institute and the church of St Giles Cripplegate were the only buildings left standing in this bomb-devastated area of the City.

GOLDSMITHS STREET EC2 (Wood Street) D3
The Hall of the Goldsmiths Company stands between Foster Lane and Gutter Lane, and the street is named after that company.

GOODMANS YARD E1 (Minories) H4
In the early sixteenth century the land to the east of modern Minories was farmland owned by Roland Goodman, a wealthy City merchant.

GOPHIR LANE EC4 (Bush Lane) E4
A City merchant named Elias Gofaire lived on this site in the early fourteenth century, and the lane is named in his memory.

GORING STREET EC3 (Bevis Marks) G3

George Goring, the Earl of Norwich, was a favourite of James I, and he played a great part in helping the King's son, Charles I, during the Civil War. Goring died in 1663 and the street is named in his honour.

GOUGH SQUARE EC4 (Bolt Court to Fleet Street) B3

The house of Nicholas Gough, a master printer, was originally situated here, and the square is named after him. This area of Fleet Street was taken up mostly by printers and publishers as indeed it is to this day. For this reason Samuel Johnson moved into number 17 Gough Square in 1748 to compile his famous dictionary, which was published in 1755. Dr Johnson was a famous figure in Fleet Street, tapping the street posts with his stick as he made his way to the Cheshire Cheese or to the Mitre; he was also a frequent visitor to the church of St Clement Danes in the Strand. A statue of Dr Johnson stands at the eastern end of St Clement Danes, looking back down the Fleet Street he loved. He died at number 8 Bolt Court in 1784, having moved into the court in 1776 after the death of his wife.

GRACECHURCH STREET EC3 (Bishopsgate) F4

The church of St Benet Grasschurch stood on the corner of Fenchurch Street, and was so called because, in medieval times, the whole of the street was taken up by the grass or herb market. The church was built in the fourteenth century, and was completely destroyed in the Fire of 1666. Sir Christopher Wren rebuilt the church but in the late nineteenth century it had become so dilapidated that it was demolished to make way for offices. To the ancient herb market came Londoners to buy healing medicines made from grass or wild plants, and in the sixteenth century hay, corn, malt, and cheese were all sold there. In 1666 the flames of the Great Fire consumed the entire street, and because of the advancement made in medicine the market disappeared for ever.

After the Fire the medieval Grascherchestrat became known as Gracious Street and after the turn of the seventeenth century acquired its present name.

GRASS COURT EC2 (Gracechurch Street) F4

The court is named in memory of the old grass market in Gracechurch Street.

GRAYS INN ROAD WC1 (Holborn Bars) A1

The fourth of the Great Inns of Court occupies the whole of the western side of Grays Inn Road, which lies outside the western perimeter of the City boundary.

In the reign of Edward I (1272–1307) the manor house of Reginald de Gray, known as the Manor of Portpoole, stood here, and in 1505 the manor and surrounding land were leased by Lord Gray de Wilton to Hugh Denny, and were subsequently leased to students of law who converted the manor into one of the Inns of Court. Francis Bacon was treasurer of the Inn in 1600 and was responsible for laying out the wonderful gardens and trees.

The Great Hall was completed in 1560 and was honoured by the visit of Queen Elizabeth I, who attended a banquet there. The Hall was badly bombed in the last war but has since been completely restored. The present chapel was completed in 1699 on the site of the original chapel, which dated back to the early fourteenth century. The Inn, which has two entrances, one in High Holborn and the other in Grays Inn Road, is divided into South Square, Grays Inn Square, and Raymonds Buildings. Portpool Lane, on the eastern side of Grays Inn Road, is named in memory of the Manor of Portpoole.

GREAT BELL ALLEY EC2 (Coleman Street) E3

The alley takes its name from a sixteenth-century tavern called The Bell, which was situated here. Great Bell Alley was bisected in the 1840s by the construction of Moorgate

Street, now known as Moorgate. The eastern section of Great Bell Alley has been renamed Telegraph Street.

GREAT ST HELENS EC3 (Bishopsgate) G3
Named after the church of St Helen, which stands at the end of the courtyard. The church is all that remains of the ancient priory of the nuns of St Helen's, founded in 1212. The old hall of the priory was removed in 1799. The church survived the Great Fire of London, and in so doing the tombs of some of the City's most famous people were preserved, for buried in the church are Sir John Crosby, owner of the celebrated Crosby Hall (see Crosby Square), who died in 1475; Sir Thomas Gresham, founder of the Royal Exchange, who died in 1579; Sir Julius Caesar, Master of the Rolls, who died in 1636; Dr Jonathan Goddard, physician to Oliver Cromwell, died 1675; and Francis Bancroft who left money for almshouses in Mile End after his death in 1726.

GREAT ST THOMAS APOSTLE EC4 (Queen Street) E4
On the northern corner of Great St Thomas Apostle, at its junction with Queen Street, can still be seen a tiny portion of the churchyard of the fourteenth-century church of St Thomas Apostle, which was destroyed in the Great Fire of 1666 and not rebuilt.

GREAT SWAN ALLEY EC2 (Moorgate) E2
A sixteenth-century tavern called the Swan gave its name to the alley, which has been cut in half by the construction of Moorgate.

GREAT TOWER STREET EC3 (Eastcheap) G4
The street leads directly to the Tower of London, from which it takes its name. At the extreme eastern end of the street, at what used to be number 48, stood an inn called the Czar's Head where, in the late seventeenth century, Peter the Great of Russia supped ale with his friends after a long day's work

Page 89 (*above*) The northern side of Ludgate Hill; the Cambridge coach is starting; (*below*) the view in 1969, from Ludgate Circus

Page 90 (*above*) The old Roman wall in St Alphage Gardens, with new blocks rising behind; (*below*) the new London Wall in its skyscraper office blocks rising above the bomb debris

in Deptford, where he was studying shipbuilding. That end of the street has been altered, for it suffered particularly badly during the bombing of London. The street in former times was known as plain Tower Street.

GREAT TRINITY LANE EC4 (Queen Victoria Street) D4
A church called Holy Trinity the Less stood in this lane; it dated from Saxon times and is mentioned by John Stow in his sixteenth-century *Survey of London* as being very old and in need of repair, and as leaning on props and stilts. The church was burnt down in the Great Fire.

On its site stands the headquarters of the world-famous Hudson's Bay Company, Beaver House, which was built in 1926 and is named in memory of the days when the demand for the beaver hat led to the financing of an expedition to Hudson's Bay, and the great forests where the beaver lived. The expedition set sail in 1688 in a 43-ton ketch called the *Nonsuch*, and returned with such a haul of beaver skins that the reigning monarch, Charles II, granted the company the sole charter of trade and commerce within the Hudson Bay Strait. This was on 2 May 1670, and the five pages of the charter are preserved in Beaver House, together with many other interesting items collected during 300 years of fur trading.

GREAT WINCHESTER STREET EC2 (Old Broad Street) F3
The Marquis of Winchester acquired the priory of the Augustinian Friars from Henry VIII when the monarch dissolved the monasteries. The marquis demolished part of the priory and built the great Winchester House on the site, and here he died in 1572, aged ninety-seven. The house was demolished in 1839 and an office block bearing that name was erected in its place. After being damaged in the bombing of 1940 Great Winchester Street was completely rebuilt, and Winchester House is remembered again in a large new office block which fronts Old Broad Street. The church of the old

priory still stands in the little courtway called Austin Friars in old Broad Street.

GREEN ARBOUR COURT EC4 (Old Bailey) C2
Green Arbour, once a bower of trees or shaded walk, occupied this site before office blocks and Holborn Viaduct station were built. Oliver Goldsmith lived at number 12 in 1758. That house was demolished in the nineteenth century to make way for Holborn Viaduct Railway Station.

GRESHAM STREET EC2 (St Martins le Grand) D2
Sir Thomas Gresham was a City merchant who founded the Royal Exchange in 1566, and also left money to found a college, which was housed in his mansion in Bishopsgate after his death and his wife's. In 1843 the college was rebuilt on the corner of Basinghall Street and four little streets were renamed to form modern Gresham Street. The portion between St Martins-le-Grand and Noble Street was called St Annes Lane, and from Noble Street to Wood Street was called Maiden Lane. The portion between Wood Street and Aldermanbury was named Lad Lane, and the last or eastern part was called Cateaton Street. Before the reforming and renaming of these streets a famous hostelry called the Swan with Two Necks stood on the corner of Lad Lane and Aldermanbury. This hostelry was the starting place for northbound stage-coaches. The Swan with Two Necks was really the Swan with Two Nicks, which refers to the two nicks or marks on the bills of swans owned by the Vintners Company.

On the corner of Guildhall Yard stands the church of St Lawrence Jewry, originally built in the early twelfth century but destroyed in the Great Fire of 1666. Sir Christopher Wren rebuilt the church in 1671–7 at a cost of £11,870 1s 9d, that being the most expensive of all the rebuilt churches in the City. The church was destroyed again in the bombing on 29 December 1940, but was completely restored by Cecil Brown in 1957 and is today the official church of the City of London. The Lord Mayor and Corporation attend a service here at Michaelmas prior to the election of a new Lord Mayor. St Lawrence Jewry is so called because it stood in an area mostly occupied by Jews who had come to the country with William the Conqueror in 1066 (see Old Jewry).

GREYFRIARS PASSAGE EC1 (Newgate Street) C3
In the early thirteenth century the whole of the northern side of Newgate was occupied by the Franciscan monastery called Grey Friars. The monastery was dissolved by Henry VIII but his son, Edward VI, converted part of the monastery into a hospital or school for poor fatherless boys, which he called Christ's Hospital; it became known as the Bluecoat School, and removed to Horsham in 1902. City of London plaques mark the sites of both these buildings in Newgate Street.

GREYSTOKE PLACE EC4 (Fetter Lane) A2
Greystoke is a corruption of Greystock, an owner of property on this site in bygone days.

GROCERS HALL COURT EC2 (Poultry) E3
The Grocers Hall stands at the end of the courtway, the main entrance being in Princes Street. The grocers or pepperers were distributors of spices as long ago as the twelfth century. In 1345 they were incorporated as the Guild of Pepperers, later to be known as Grocers. Their first Hall was built on the present site in 1427 but this building was destroyed in the Great Fire of 1666, though they were fortunate that many of their early records were saved. A new Hall was built and part of it was used by the Bank of England from 1690 until 1743 when the bank erected its own premises on the corner of Threadneedle Street. The present Grocers Hall was opened in 1893 and the company, which ranks number two in precedence among the City livery companies, has supplied no fewer than 109 of their members to fill the office of Lord Mayor of London.

93

GUILDHALL BUILDINGS EC2 (Basinghall Street) E3

In this passageway, which runs between the entrance to the Guildhall and Basinghall Street, stands the City of London court. At the western end, near Guildhall Yard, stands the Irish Chamber, the committee rooms of that section of the corporation which looks after the City's estates in Coleraine and Londonderry in Ireland.

GUILDHALL YARD EC2 (Gresham Street) E3

The Guildhall has stood at the end of the Yard since the twelfth century, although the present building dates from 1411. The Great Hall has been used to entertain royal and other important visitors for nearly six centuries; it is also used for the election of the Lord Mayor and officers of the City. The Guildhall was partly destroyed in the Great Fire of London and repaired by Wren, but it was considerably altered by George Dance in the eighteenth century. It was again badly damaged on 29 December 1940, this time by enemy bombing, the roof being completely destroyed. On entering the porch of the now completely restored hall the first thing that strikes the eye are the banners of the twelve great livery companies, which, in order of precedence, are: Mercers, Grocers, Drapers, Fishmongers, Goldsmiths, Skinners, Merchant Taylors, Haberdashers, Salters, Ironmongers, Vintners, and Clothworkers. There are also monuments to Wellington, Nelson, William Pitt, and Sir Winston Churchill. At the western end of the Hall are the figures of the giants Gog and Magog, the recent work of David Evans, the original and much larger figures having been lost in the bombing of 1940. Gogmagog and Corineus were the legendary Britons who repelled the Trojans from these shores 1,000 years before the coming of the Romans; Corineus has been forgotten, and Gogmagog has somehow over the centuries become a pair of giants. The original figures were carved in 1708 by a local craftsman named Richard Saunders, and they measured 14 ft 6 in high, compared with the new figures which measure 9 ft 3 in.

On the eastern side of Guildhall Yard are the Art Gallery and Library. The Guildhall Library was founded in 1425 but was demolished in 1550. The present library was built in 1872 and is one of the finest reference libraries in London, specialising in works on London, Middlesex, and English history, with a collection of nearly 140,000 volumes. A plaque marks the site of the original library. A plaque also marks the site of the old Guildhall chapel (1299–1822), which occupied the eastern side of Guildhall Yard, adjacent to the Great Hall.

Another plque on the eastern side marks the site of Black-well Hall, the home of Sir Ralph Blackwell, which stood here until 1820 when it was demolished to make way for the City Bankruptcy Court.

GUNPOWDER ALLEY EC4 (Shoe Lane) B3

In the late seventeenth century when the reign of Charles II was ending, there was fear among Londoners that the king's brother, the future James II, would restore the Catholic faith and all over England no-popery meetings were held; and none were larger than those held in Fleet Street where effigies of the Pope were burned or blown up. The gunpowder used in the demonstrations were made and stored in the little courtway which was nicknamed Gunpowder Alley.

Richard Lovelace, the poet, died in the alley in 1658.

GUTTER LANE EC2 (Cheapside) D3

A family named Gutherun were tenants of property in the lane in the eleventh century, and for a few hundred years the lane was called Gutherons Lane, of which the present name is a corruption. The lane was completely destroyed in the bombing of 1940, and is now rebuilt with large office blocks on either side. At the extreme north-eastern end is the Hall of the Wax Chandlers Company, which has occupied the site for 600 years. The Hall was completely destroyed in the bombing of 1940 and during excavations in 1957 for the

95

building of a new Hall some perfect examples of Roman pottery were found. These are now kept in the Guildhall museum. Next to Wax Chandlers Hall is a very popular City eating house called the Baron of Beef.

At the south-eastern end is the newly built Hall of the Saddlers Company, which was incorporated in 1363. This company still trains young men to inspect the saddles and harnesses made in the London area, to ensure that they are of the finest quality. The old Hall, rebuilt in 1822, was also obliterated in the bombing of December 1940.

HALF MOON COURT EC1 (Bartholomew Close) D2
This court formerly led to the tavern called the Half Moon, which stood in Aldersgate Street; the tavern was popular in the sixteenth century with the acting fraternity, and it is believed that William Shakespeare once lived there. It was demolished in 1879 to make way for City improvements.

HAMMET STREET EC3 (Minories) H4
Sir Benjamin Hammet, a partner in the City bank of Esdaile, Hammet, Esdaile, was elected alderman of the Portsoken Ward in the late eighteenth century. Hammet Street, which was named after him, was completely destroyed in the bombing of World War II, and is now being rebuilt.

HANGING SWORD ALLEY EC4 (Whitefriars Street) B3
A fourteenth-century tavern called the Hanging Sword stood here, and the alley took its name from that tavern. Previously the alley was known as Blood Bowl Alley from an earlier inn of that name.

HARE COURT EC4 (Middle Temple Lane) A3
Sir Nicholas Hare was Privy Councillor to Henry VIII, and became Master of the Rolls in the reign of Queen Mary I. The court was named in his memory when he died in 1557.

HARE PLACE EC4 (Fleet Street) A3

The sixteenth-century mansion of Sir Nicholas Hare stood on this site. When the house was demolished the alley was called Ram Alley, and became one of the City's most notorious sanctuaries for thieves and the riffraff of Fleet Street. The alley was closed by an Act of Parliament in the reign of William and Mary, the slums and taverns were cleared, and a new thoroughfare was formed and named in honour of Sir Nicholas Hare.

HARP ALLEY EC4 (Farringdon Street) B3

A seventeenth-century inn called the Harp stood in this alley. In the early eighteenth century when every City shop or professional residence had its own sign hanging outside (houses were not numbered in those days) a Dutchman named Vandertrout owned a signboard manufactory, situated in this alley.

HARP LANE EC3 (Lower Thames Street) G5

The lane is named after a tavern called Le Harpe which stood in Great Tower Street (near Harp Lane) in the sixteenth century. In Harp Lane stands the Hall of the Bakers Company, incorporated in 1486. The old Bakers Hall was obliterated in the bombing of 1940, but a new one has been recently erected on the same site. The Company was responsible for maintaining a regular price for a standard loaf.

HARROW PLACE E1 (Middlesex Street) H2

Harrow Place is a reminder of the sixteenth century when the whole of this eastern area outside the City wall was still countryside. Middlesex Street, or Petticoat Lane as it is better known, was itself then called Hog Lane, from the pig farms in the area. The Harrow was a popular inn sign for taverns situated near farmland.

HART STREET EC3 (Mark Lane) G4

The church of St Olave, on the southern side of the street, has stood here since Saxon times, when it received its dedication from the Norwegian sea king Olave, who assisted King Ethelred II in his fight against the Danes in the tenth century. Many years ago a few pieces of the old church plate were found, and these were engraved with tiny hearts, probably the emblem of the original church. These hearts are said to have led to the origination of the street's name. The present church, one of the few to escape the flames of the Great Fire of 1666, dates back to at least 1319, although it was considerably restored after the bombing of 1940. King Haakon of Norway laid the foundation stone at the start of the restoration in 1954. The church has strong associations with Samuel Pepys, the diarist, who lived in nearby Seething Lane, and both he and his wife are buried in it. Also buried in the churchyard were hundreds of victims of the plague of 1665. A gateway in Seething Lane has over its porch some small plaster skulls, which were put there during the plague to warn people that this was the gate of death.

In the sixteenth century Hart Street was inhabited by some of the City's wealthiest people. Sir John Allen, who was Lord Mayor in 1525, built his mansion here, and this was later occupied by Sir Francis Walsingham. Another old mansion which stood in Hart Street in the sixteenth century was called Whittington's Palace, and is said to have been the old home of Richard Whittington, Lord Mayor of London.

HARTSHORN ALLEY EC3 (Fenchurch Street) G3

A medieval inn whose sign was the horns of the hart, the male red deer, a common sight in the forests of Essex, stood on this site.

HATTON GARDEN EC1 (Holborn Circus) B2

The history of Hatton Garden lies in the tiny private terrace

98

called Ely Place, at the western end of Charterhouse Street near Holborn Circus, which runs parallel with Hatton Garden. Ely Place had been since the late thirteenth century the London home of the Bishops of Ely, and was also a Catholic sanctuary.

When Queen Elizabeth I came to the throne one of her favourites was Christopher Hatton whom she had met whilst he was studying law at the Middle Temple. Handsome and a good dancer, Hatton in a few years was knighted and made Lord Chancellor. In 1576 Richard Cox, the Bishop of Ely, was persuaded by the Protestant Elizabeth to hand over a large portion of Ely Place and about 14 acres of orchard land to Sir Christopher Hatton, who borrowed large sums of money from the Queen to develop the land. Sir Christopher Hatton, known as the dancing Lord Chancellor, died in Ely Place in 1591. There are streets in the neighbourhood of Hatton Garden which today remind us of the days when the area was his orchard land—Vine Street, Plum Tree Court and Saffron Hill. In Mitre Court, at the southeastern end of Hatton Garden is the old Mitre Tavern; a stump of a cherry tree still stands in the middle of the bar as a reminder of the days when strawberries and cherries were cultivated here.

In Ely Place there still stands the old chapel of the Bishops of Ely, built between 1290 and 1298 and now once again the private property of the Catholic church. The chapel, called St Ethelreda's, was partially destroyed in the bombing of London, but it has now been completely restored.

Hatton Garden lies just outside the City boundary, and is today the centre of Britain's diamond trade; and diamond merchants can be seen conducting their business on every corner of the 'Garden'.

HELMET COURT EC2 (Wormwood Street) G2
The helmet of the medieval soldier was a favourite inn sign, and an inn of that name stood on this site.

HEN AND CHICKEN COURT EC4 (Fleet Street) A3
For centuries Fleet Street has been famous for its numerous taverns, and here stood a tavern called the Hen and Chicken.

HENEAGE LANE (Bevis Marks) G3
The old mansion of the abbots of Bury St Edmunds, which stood in Bevis Marks, almost opposite the lane, passed into the hands of Thomas Heneage in the early sixteenth century, and the lane perpetuates his name.

HIGH TIMBER STREET EC4 (Upper Thames Street) D4
The Fishmongers Company owned much of the land on this stretch of the waterfront, for in the thirteenth century this part of the river front was given to the company by the Dean and Chapter of St Paul's for the unloading of the timber from which the fish boxes were made.

HIND COURT EC4 (Fleet Street) B3
Another of Fleet Street's many inns stood on this site, its sign that of the female red deer or hind, a popular inn sign in the sixteenth century when deer still roamed the forests of what is now north-east London.

HOGARTH COURT EC3 (Fenchurch Street) G4
The court is probably named after William Hogarth, the great painter, who became famous for his works on the everyday life of the City of London. William Hogarth and his wife are buried in the church of St Nicholas in Chiswick.

HOLBORN EC1 A2
Holborn or Hol-Burne was the name given to that part of the old River Fleet that flowed under what is now Holborn Viaduct, and is now covered over by modern Farringdon Street. Holborn, then, is really the burne or river in the hollow, the hollow being the valley at the eastern end of Holborn, now spanned by Holborn Viaduct.

Prisoners leaving Newgate prison bound for the hanging tree at Tyburn (now Marble Arch) were forced to walk up Holborn Hill and it was they who gave it the name Heavy Hill. The western end of Holborn is also the western end of the City boundary, and is known as Holborn Bars. On the southern side at the western end, and lying outside the boundary, can be seen a row of sixteenth-century houses called Staple Inn, and these houses give one a good idea of what Holborn looked like in the reign of Elizabeth I.

On the northern side is the huge red-brick building of the Prudential Assurance Company which occupies the site of Furnivals Inn, demolished in 1897. On the same side is the old-established popular store of Gamage's. Opposite Gamage's, on the corner of New Fetter Lane, stands the offices of the *Daily Mirror*, one of Britain's best-selling daily newspapers; a great glass building completed in the early 1960s, it is said to be the largest newspaper office in Britain.

HOLBORN CIRCUS EC1 B2

Holborn Circus was built in the 1870s in the general improvement of the Holborn valley. In the middle of the circus is an equestrian statue of Albert, consort to Queen Victoria.

HOLBORN VIADUCT EC1 B2

Towards the middle of the nineteenth century, with the increase in wheeled traffic the steep incline of Holborn Hill became a hazard, especially in winter. People would gather just to watch horses and carts get out of control whilst climbing or descending Heavy Hill, as it was christened by the prisoners of Newgate. In 1863 the bridging of the Holborn valley was begun, and six years later, on 6 November 1869, Holborn Viaduct was completed, the opening ceremony being performed by Queen Victoria. Four bronze statues dedicated to Commerce, Agriculture, Science, and Art adorned the bridge, and on the buildings at the four corners of the bridge were respectively the statues of Sir Hugh Middleton

(1555–1631), the man who first piped drinking water into the City; Sir William Walworth, Lord Mayor of London, who slew Wat Tyler, the leader of the Peasants' Revolt in nearby Smithfield in 1381; Henry Fitz Ailwyne, the City's first and longest serving Lord Mayor (from 1189 to 1212); and Sir Thomas Gresham (1519–79), founder of the Royal Exchange. The viaduct was damaged in the bombing of 1941, and the statues of Sir Hugh Middleton and Sir William Walworth were swept away in the blast.

The viaduct is over 1,800 ft long and 80 ft wide, and cost over £2,500,000 to build. A host of little streets were demolished to make way for it, among them two of the City's most notorious slums, Skinner Street and Field Lane, where thousands of handkerchiefs, purchased from pickpockets, were on sale.

On the southern side of the viaduct is the church of St Andrew, which has stood here from at least the thirteenth century. The old church escaped the Great Fire of London, but being in a state of decay it was rebuilt by Sir Christopher Wren in 1686, only to be destroyed again in the bombing of 1941. The church has now been completely restored and its register, which was saved, records the christening of the great statesman Benjamin Disraeli on 31 July 1817, aged twelve years.

Next door to St Andrew's is the City Temple, first founded in 1640, but like St Andrews damaged in the bombing of 1941 and restored, in 1958. The City Temple is a Congregationalist church and is known as the cathedral of free churches.

On the northern side is the famous church of St Sepulchre, which was founded in the twelfth century but consumed in the very last flames of the Great Fire of London, which came to a halt just round the corner in Giltspur Street, at the corner of Cock Lane, or Pie Corner as it was then known. The parishioners of St Sepulchre's could not wait for the church to be rebuilt so they set about the job themselves from a design by Wren, to whom is attributed the rebuilding of the centre of the church in 1670. One of the most famous vicars of the church was John Rogers, who was burnt at the stake in Smithfield in front of his family for his Protestant beliefs—the first Protestant martyr during the reign of Queen Mary I. The church has long associations with Newgate prison which stood opposite (Old Bailey), and every midnight before the next day's execution, a hand bell, which can still be seen in the church, was rung to announce the forthcoming execution. Each prisoner was handed a bunch of flowers before he set off for the hanging tree at Tyburn (Marble Arch).

In the church is buried Captain John Smith, the leader of the settlers in Virginia, who died in 1631. Also buried in the church is Roger Ascham, Queen Elizabeth I's tutor, who died in 1568. There is a monument to Sir Henry Wood, the founder of the Promenade Concerts; he first learnt to play the organ in this church.

HONEY LANE EC2 (Cheapside) E3

In medieval times, before sugar was refined, the housewife bought natural honey from the beekeepers whose shops stood in Honey Lane. A church called All Hallows, Honey Lane, was completely destroyed in the Great Fire of 1666, and on its site a marketplace was erected. Honey Lane market itself was demolished to make way for the City of London school, which was opened on 2 February 1837.

HOOD COURT EC4 (Fleet Street) B3

Thomas Hood, the poet, was born in Poultry in 1799 in a bookshop owned by his father. Hood, in the early days of magazines and periodicals, founded a paper called *Hood's Magazine*, and it is fitting that he is remembered in Fleet Street, the world of journalism. He died in 1845 and is buried in Kensal Green cemetery.

HOSIER LANE EC1 (West Smithfield) C2

In the fourteenth century long hose became the fashion with men, and the manufacturers of hose lived mainly in this little lane, which today forms part of Smithfield market and is lost in the mass of meat warehouses and office blocks.

HOUNDSDITCH EC3 (Bishopsgate) G2

In Saxon times a ditch or moat ran outside the City wall, but over the centuries the moat was gradually filled in until only the stretch known today as Houndsditch was left. Into this filthy strip of water were thrown all the dead domestic animals, which led to it being called Hounds Ditch or Dogs Ditch. The ditch was finally filled in and paved in the year 1503 and the newly paved street was immediately occupied by Jewish secondhand-clothes merchants. The area today is still occupied mainly by Jews, as can be seen on Sundays when nearby Petticoat Lane market is in operation.

Houndsditch is certainly unique in having at both ends a church dedicated to St Botolph.

HUGGIN HILL EC4 (Queen Victoria Street) D4

Huggin Hill was formerly called Spuren Lane, the name being derived from the fact that most of the spur makers lived there. The reason the name was changed is obscure, but could be attributed to the fact that pigs were kept in this area and that the name is a corruption of Hoggen Lane.

IDOL LANE EC3 (Eastcheap) F4

The makers of idols or tiny statuettes lived in this lane, and their craft has lived for centuries in its name.

On the eastern side of Idol Lane can be seen the shell of one of the City's most famous churches, St Dunstan-in-the-East, so named to distinguish it from the church of St Dunstan-in-the-West which stands in Fleet Street. St Dunstan's has occupied this site since Saxon times. It was rebuilt in the fourteenth century only to be destroyed in the Great

Fire of London. Sir Christopher Wren rebuilt it in 1679, but it was not to his usual high standard, and it was found necessary to rebuild it once again 1817, when the tower was all that was kept of Wren's work. The church was shattered in May 1941 by the bombs which devastated the eastern end of Eastcheap, but again Wren's tower survived, and it stands to this day.

INDIA STREET EC3 (Minories) H4

India Street, like nearby Rangoon Street, is named after the East India Company, whose great house occupied the site in Leadenhall Street where Lloyd's, the great shipping insurance building, now stands. Britain began trading with the East Indies in the late sixteenth century, when silks, spices, and ivory were in demand. A company formed to trade with the East Indies was incorporated by James I in 1609, and in 1726 the company erected a huge building on the corner of Lime Street and Leadenhall Street called East India House. The house was one of the sights of the City, and people came from far and near to see the treasures acquired in 150 years of trading with the East Indies. In 1858, when trouble and mutiny in India had reduced trade, the East India Company passed to the Crown, and in 1862 the great East India House was demolished and the company's treasures were exhibited in the Indian Museum in Whitehall.

INGRAM COURT EC3 (Fenchurch Street) F4

Sir Arthur Ingram was a well-known city merchant and a benefactor to the church of St Dionis Backchurch, that stood near Lime Street, a little back from Fenchurch Street (see page 68). The church, rebuilt by Wren after the Great Fire of 1666, was demolished in 1878 to make way for a new office block.

INNER TEMPLE LANE EC4 (Fleet Street) A3

The Knights Templars were formed in the early twelfth century to escort and protect pilgrims journeying to the Holy Land. In 1184 the Templars built their headquarters near the Thames, dividing themselves into three sections, the Inner, Middle, and Outer Temples. In 1312 the Order of Knights Templars was dissolved, and in 1323 their headquarters passed into the hands of the Order of St John, who leased the Inner and Middle Temples to the students of law. The old Outer Temple was granted to Walter de Stapeldon, the Bishop of Exeter, who erected Exeter House on the site (see Essex Court). The students of law have, over the centuries, built upon the old site, but have remembered the original owners by dividing their building into two halls, the Inner and Outer Temples, and naming the whole site The Temple. The entrance to the Inner Temple is via the Inner Temple Gate, which was rebuilt in 1748.

The buildings on either side of Inner Temple Lane are called Dr Johnsons Buildings, in memory of the great man who lived here from 1760 to 1765. On the opposite side of the lane Goldsmiths Buildings perpetuate the name of Oliver Goldsmith, who lived here from 1768 until his death in 1774.

At the end of Inner Temple Lane stands the original church of the old Knights Templars, built in round form to emulate the Holy Sepulchre in Jerusalem. The church, built in 1185 and dedicated to St Mary the Virgin, was very badly bombed in 1941, but has since been completely restored by Walter H. Godfrey, and was reopened in 1958. Nine of the effigies of the old Knights Templars can still be seen in the church. On the eastern side of the church is the Master's House of the Temple, which has also been rebuilt since the bombing. South of the church lies the Inner Temple Hall; the original Hall where the knights dined and entertained their guests was rebuilt in 1870, but was destroyed in 1941 by enemy bombs, and the new Hall was opened in 1955, the foundation stone having been laid by Queen Elizabeth II in 1952.

Page 107 (*above*) Temple Bar and The Devil Tavern; (*below*) 'The Griffin', marking the site of the old Temple Bar

Page 108   (above) St Paul's from Fleet Street; (below) St Paul's with its new neighbours

IRONMONGER LANE EC2 (Cheapside) E3

Up to the early fifteenth century the ironmongers of the City lived and worked chiefly in Ironmonger Lane and neighbouring Old Jewry, and they moved to Fenchurch Street in 1457.

On the eastern side of the lane stands the Hall of the premier City livery company, the Mercers or traders in textiles. The hall stands on the site formerly occupied by the house of Gilbert à Becket, the father of Thomas à Becket, the martyr, who was born in the house in 1119. The house was eventually demolished and a hospital called St Thomas Acon was built on its site. The Mercers Company, which had been incorporated in 1393, was granted the hospital by Henry VIII, and here built its Hall and chapel. The original Hall was destroyed in the Great Fire of 1666 and a new one was built, only to be destroyed again by enemy bombs in 1941. Sir Richard Whittington, four times Lord Mayor of London, was a Master of the Mercers Company and today the company is responsible for looking after the estates bequeathed by him, and also the Whittington College in Highgate.

On the eastern side of Ironmonger Lane stood a very old church called St Martin Pomeroy, so called because it stood on the site of an old apple orchard. The church was destroyed in the Fire of 1666 and was not rebuilt.

JEWRY STREET EC3 (Crutched Friars) H3

Jews came to England with William the Conqueror in 1066 and settled mainly in a ghetto near West Cheap (Cheapside). In 1290 King Edward I banished all Jews from England for usury and for debasing the coinage. They stayed out of England for three and a half centuries, and did not return until the 'Protector', Cromwell, granted them permission. This time they found a new home near the Tower of London, and Jewry Street is named in their memory. In modern Jewry Street stands the Sir John Cass College, founded by the eighteenth-century benefactor of that name who was alderman of the Portsoken Ward in which Jewry Street lies. The college was built in 1898 from money left for the purpose by Sir John Cass.

JOHN CARPENTER STREET EC4 (Tudor Street) B4

John Carpenter was Town Clerk of London in the early fifteenth century; he left money for the education of poor boys, and instructed that certain properties be sold in order to help that aim. In 1837 the City of London school was erected, with money raised from the bequest, on the site of Honey Lane market in Milk Street. In 1881 the school was dismantled and re-erected on its present site at the corner of John Carpenter Street and Queen Victoria Embankment.

On the western side of John Carpenter Street stands the Guildhall School of Music, built in 1857 for the teaching of music and the education of actors and actresses. Dame Myra Hess and Dame Sybil Thorndyke studied there.

JOHNSONS COURT EC4 (Fleet Street) B3

An Elizabethan merchant tailor named Johnson owned this property and the court is named after him; 200 years later his namesake, Dr Johnson, moved into number 7 Johnsons Court, where he edited his edition of Shakespeare. At number 11 the first edition of the City magaine *John Bull* was printed in 1820, its editor and founder being Theodore Hook.

KING EDWARD STREET ECI (Newgate Street) C3

King Edward VI granted a portion of the old Greyfriars monastery, which had been dissolved by his father Henry VIII, for the building of a school called Christ's Hospital, which stood on the northern side of Newgate Street as late as 1902.

On the north-western side of King Edward Street is the great General Post Office building, and in front of the main entrance is a statue of Sir Rowland Hill, the man who reformed the postal system and introduced the penny post in 1840.

At the south-western end of the street stands the shell of Wren's Christ Church, which was gutted in the bombing of 1940, and still awaits rebuilding.

King Edward Street was formerly called Stinking Lane from the smells of decaying meat on the butchers' stalls which stood in Newgate Street. During excavations here in the late nineteenth century part of an old Roman cemetery was found.

KING STREET EC2 (Cheapside) E3

Prior to the Great Fire of 1666 the only means of access to the Guildhall was via Lawrence Lane or Ironmonger Lane. The destruction of this part of Cheapside provided an opportunity to build a direct access to the Guildhall, and the newly erected street was named in honour of Charles II, the reigning monarch.

KING WILLIAM STREET EC4 (London Bridge) F4

King William Street was built in 1830, to form another direct approach to the newly built London Bridge, and to ease traffic congestion in that area. In 1831 the extreme end of Eastcheap was demolished for this purpose, and a statue of the reigning monarch, William IV, was erected on the site of the famous Boars Head tavern (see Eastcheap). The statue was destroyed in the bombing, and has not been replaced.

At the junction of King William and Lombard Streets stands the church of St Mary Woolnoth, which is said to stand on the site of an old Roman temple of Concord. The name Woolnoth is derived from the builder of the first church, a Saxon named Wulfnoth. The church was rebuilt in the reign of William the Conqueror, and again in 1445 by the Goldsmiths Company, in particular by Sir Martin Bowes-Lyon, a member of that company whose banners still hang by the organ. Queen Elizabeth, the Queen Mother is a descendant of the family. The church was destroyed in the Fire of 1666 and restored by Sir Christopher Wren; it was completely rebuilt by Wren's pupil, Nicholas Hawksmoor, between 1716 and 1727. St Mary Woolnoth was fortunate in escaping the bombing of 1941 but the clergy of the church witnessed one of the saddest sights of the bombing: a bomb scored a direct hit on the entrance to the Bank underground station, and the blast reverberated down the tunnel, forcing a huge hole in the roadway in front of St Mary Woolnoth through which were blasted the bodies of people seeking shelter from the bombing. Bodies, like tailors' dummies, were thrown up into the air on to the debris of the wrecked buildings outside. The crypt of the church was sold to London Transport in the early 1900s in order that the Bank underground station could be built, and it is the only church in London that stands on a railway station. The present church has been lent to German-speaking Swiss people residing in or visiting London, and it is also the official London church for British Colombia.

KINGS BENCH WALK EC4 (Inner Temple) A3
The Kings Bench office that stood on this site contained all the court records, but the buildings were destroyed by fire in 1677. Sir Christopher Wren rebuilt part of the Walk. Oliver Goldsmith lived at number 3 Kings Bench Walk in 1765.

KINGSCOTE STREET EC4 (Tudor Street) B4
Bridewell Palace, the residence of Henry VIII and Katharine of Aragon, occupied the whole of this area. The palace was granted to the City corporation by Henry's son, Edward VI, in 1553, and was converted into a prison and workhouse. The buildings were eventually demolished in 1864 and the present street pattern was formed. Kingscote Street was formerly King Edward Street, in memory of Edward VI, the last owner of Bridewell Palace, but owing to the increasing

number of streets bearing that name in the City, the name was changed to Kings *Cote*, implying that the king has passed or been near this place.

KINGSHEAD COURT EC3 (Fish Street Hill) F4

A sixteenth-century tavern whose sign was the head of Henry VIII stood on this site until it was destroyed in the Great Fire of 1666.

KNIGHTRIDER STREET EC4 (Godliman Street) C4

In the twelfth century knights in armour rode from King Stephen's Palace, called Tower Royal which stood in Cannon Street, to the jousting fields of Smithfield, and their route from the Palace, where crowds gathered to watch them, was called Knightrider Street. The extreme eastern end of Knightrider Street, called Old Fish Street, was the earliest fish market in the City, and was demolished when Queen Victoria Street was cut through the City. The bombing of London has altered the area even more, and only a small section of the original knights' route is now left. At number 5 lived Thomas Linacre, the physician to Henry VII, Henry VIII, and Queen Mary I before she was queen; in that house he founded, in 1518, the Royal College of Physicians.

On the site occupied by the newly built Old Change Court stood the church of St Mary Magdalen. Dating from Saxon times, it was destroyed in the Great Fire of London and rebuilt by Sir Christopher Wren, badly damaged by fire in 1866, and was sold and demolished in 1887.

On the site now occupied by Faraday buildings stood Doctors Commons, the building consisting of five courts set up in the reign of Queen Elizabeth I to issue marriage licences and to store wills and testaments. There was also a court of dispensation, which could sanction reasonable requests to break the law in some specific instance. Here, too, was the office of the Lord High Admiral of England. The Doctors Commons was demolished in 1867 to make way for the building of Queen Victoria Street, and is commemorated by a plaque on Faraday Buildings.

LAMBETH HILL EC4 (Queen Victoria Street) D4

In the early thirteenth century a family named Lamberd owned property on this site, and the hill leading to their house was known as *Lamberdshelle*. Near Lambeth Hill stood a church called St Mary Mounthaw, named after a local family who must have been of some importance; the church was one of the eighty-nine consumed by the Great Fire of London.

LANGBOURN CHANCERY EC3 (Fenchurch Street) F4

According to Stow in his sixteenth-century *Survey of London*, the Ward of Langbourn takes its name from a stream of that name which flowed along Fenchurch Street to Lombard Street to join the River Walbrook near the Mansion House. This is considered to be incorrect by modern historians because, apart from the fact that no trace has ever been found of the stream, Stow's suggested course flows uphill. A modern theory is that the Ward was named after the Longobards, or Lombards, the bankers of Lombard Street. Langbourn Chancery marks the site of the old chancery or records house of the Ward.

LAURENCE POUNTNEY HILL EC4 (Cannon Street) E4

The church of St Lawrence Pountney stood on this hill; it incorporated a college founded by Sir John Pountney, three times Lord Mayor of London in the early fourteenth century. The church was destroyed in the Great Fire of London and not rebuilt. Sir John Pountney's house stood here and was known as Pountney's Inn, later becoming known as the Manor of the Rose, and mentioned under that name in Shakespeare's *Henry VIII*. The house was later demolished and Suffolk House, the home of the Dukes of Suffolk, was erected on the site. Ducksfoot Lane at the southern end of Laurence

Pountney Hill is really Dukes Foot Lane, that is the footway from the river to the Duke of Suffolk's house. After passing into the hands of other noblemen the house was finally sold to the Merchant Taylors Company, which built its school there, where it remained until being removed to the Charterhouse in 1873.

LAURENCE POUNTNEY LANE EC4 (Cannon Street) E4
Named after Sir John Pountney who was Lord Mayor of London in 1330, 1331, and 1333. His house stood on the hill adjacent to the lane which perpetuates his name.

LAWRENCE LANE EC2 (Cheapside) E3
Before the Fire of 1666 Lawrence Lane was the main access to the church of St Lawrence Jewry standing in Gresham Street. The lane was completely destroyed in the bombing of London, and has been rebuilt and slightly reformed, having lost both its northern and southern ends, and so no longer connecting Cheapside with Gresham Street.

LEADENHALL MARKET EC3 (Gracechurch Stre et) F3
In 1309 Sir Hugh Neville built his mansion here, giving it a lead roof, which earned it the name Leaden Hall, and eventually the street in which the mansion stood was named Leadenhall Street. In the early fifteenth century the hall was acquired by Sir Richard Whittington, who granted it to the City corporation. In 1445 the Lord Mayor, Sir Simon Eyre, converted it into a granary and marketplace. The market grew, and in 1730 was completely rebuilt as a meat market; it was rebuilt again in 1881 at a cost of £99,000. In 1922 a part of an old Roman forum was discovered beneath the market, and it is believed that ruins of the Roman administration building lie beneath it also.

LEADENHALL STREET EC3 (Bishopsgate) F3
Named after the lead-roofed hall of Sir Hugh Neville, which

was built in 1309 on the site now occupied by Leadenhall market. On the site now occupied by Lloyd's Insurance Building stood East India House, the headquarters of the East India Company, incorporated by James I in 1609 to trade with the East Indies. In 1726 East India House was erected on the western corner of Lime Street, and in the great house were exhibited many of the treasures acquired through the Company's years of trading. Charles Lamb was a clerk in East India House from 1792 until 1825.

At the corner of St Mary Axe (page 179) stands the church of St Andrew Undershaft, which has occupied this site since the first church was built in Saxon times. The name Undershaft was acquired in medieval days when, on May Day, a shaft or maypole higher than the steeple of St Andrew was raised in Leadenhall Street (see St Mary Axe).

At the eastern end of the street stands the church of St Katherine Cree (*cree* being a medieval word for Christ). The church was built in the late thirteenth century within the precincts of the priory of Holy Trinity, Christchurch, which occupied the whole of the eastern end of Leadenhall Street (see Creechurch Lane). St Katherine Cree was rebuilt in 1631 and was one of the eight churches in the City to escape the Great Fire. In the church is buried Sir Nicholas Throgmorton who died in 1571, and who gave his name to Throgmorton Street.

Modern Leadenhall Street is given over to the shipping industry, and the offices of many of the great shipping lines are to be found at the eastern end.

LIME STREET EC3 (Leadenhall Street) G3

In medieval days the lime burners of the City made and sold lime to be used in the building of houses in this street. In the twelfth century the street was known as limstrate.

Both sides of modern Lime Street are occupied by the great buildings of Lloyd's Insurance, which were erected in 1928. Lloyd's started off as a marine insurance company, founded in the late seventeenth century in a coffee house in Great Tower Street, near the Tower of London, owned by Edward Lloyd. Lloyd then moved into another coffee house in Lombard Street on the corner of Abchurch Lane. In 1770, seeking larger premises to house the expanding marine insurance company, Lloyd moved into Popes Head Alley, and in 1774 the company moved into the Royal Exchange, where it stayed until its own offices were erected in Lime Street in 1928. Lloyd's are the world's premier shipping insurers and, inside the building, the movement of the world's ships is posted up daily. Any mishaps to ships insured by the company are posted in the 'Chamber of Horrors', and traditionally the great Lutine bell is rung to command silence for announcements affecting shipping. In 1926 the company undertook all other forms of insurance—fire, theft, accident, insurance against the arrival of twins—and today it is one of the world's largest insurance companies. The Lloyd's *Register of Shipping* is housed in another building in Fenchurch Street, at the corner of Lloyd's Avenue.

LITTLE BRITAIN EC1 (West Smithfield) C2

The Duke of Brittany came to England with William the Conqueror and Bretons settled here. In the early fourteenth century John, Duke of Brittany, built a fine mansion in this street which was called Duck Lane. The name was changed to Peti Bretane, and later to its present form.

From the fifteenth to the early eighteenth centuries Little Britain was the centre of the City's book trade, the whole street filled with the shops and houses of publishers and booksellers. It was in this street that the Earl of Dorset, rummaging through some books and papers in a secondhand bookshop, came across an unknown work called *Paradise Lost*, written by an author named John Milton; the Earl took the work to John Dryden who recognised its genius, and the book was published in 1667. John Milton had in fact lodged in Little Britain in the house of a secondhand bookseller in about 1662. Little Britain lost its trade to Paternoster Row at the beginning of the eighteenth century. The western side of Little Britain is taken up by St Bartholomew's Hospital (see Giltspur Street).

At the north-eastern end, at its junction with West Smithfield, a passageway leads to the church of St Bartholomew the Great, the oldest church in the City. Rahere, court jester to Henry I, founded a priory dedicated to St Bartholomew in 1123, and the present church, which is only a portion of the original, is the last trace of this. The priory was dissolved in 1539 by Henry VIII and sold to Sir Richard Rich, whose family held the property until the early nineteenth century. Inside the church can be seen the tomb of Rahere, the founder, who died in 1143; also, on a window, can be seen a rebus of Prior Bolton (a crossbow bolt piercing a tun or beer cask) who had carried out considerable restoration to the church in 1520. There is a monument to Sir Walter Mildmay, Chancellor of the Exchequer to Queen Elizabeth I, and one of the judges at the trial of Mary Queen of Scots.

LITTLE NEW STREET EC4 (Shoe Lane) B3
In the early sixteenth century the whole of this area was left to the Goldsmiths Company by Agnes Harding. The company developed the area and Little New Street was so named because it was the smallest of the new streets.

LITTLE SOMERSET STREET E1 (Aldgate High Street) H3
In Aldgate High Street, on the corner of Little Somerset Street, stood a large old house belonging to the Beauforts, the Dukes of Somerset. The house was demolished in 1882, and Little Somerset Street was named in the dukes' honour.

LITTLE TRINITY LANE EC4 (Upper Thames Street) D4
The church of Holy Trinity the Less stood at the northern end of the lane. The church, dating from Saxon times, is described by John Stow in his sixteenth-century *Survey of*

London, as standing on stilts, and being in need of repair. The church was destroyed in the Great Fire of London, and was not rebuilt. Beaver House, the offices of the Hudson's Bay Company, now occupies the site (see Great Trinity Lane).

On the western side of Little Trinity Lane stands the Painters Hall. The Painters and Stainers Company existed in the fourteenth century and was incorporated by Queen Elizabeth I. Sir Christopher Wren rebuilt the Hall after the fire of 1666, and the building was again considerably restored after the bombing of the last war.

LIVERPOOL STREET EC2 (Bishopsgate) G2

On the site now occupied by Liverpool Street station was erected in 1246 a priory dedicated to the Star of Bethlehem. The priory was dissolved by Henry VIII, and was granted to the City Corporation who converted it into a hospital for the insane. Bethlehem Hospital, corrupted through the years to *Bedlam Hospital*, stood here until 1676, taking in the City's lunatics. Patients who were partly cured were released—to be called Tom O'Bedlams by the City folk. In 1676 Bedlam was removed to London Wall, near Moorgate, houses and gardens were built on the site, and the street was then named Old Bethlehem in memory of the hospital. In 1829 the street was widened and named Liverpool Street after Lord Liverpool, and in 1863 the whole area was cleared in preparation for the building of the Great Eastern railway station. The station was opened in 1875 and named Liverpool Street after Lord Liverpool, Prime Minister during the period 1812–27. Broad Street station was owned by the old North London Railway Company, and was built to serve the north London suburbs.

LLOYDS AVENUE EC3 (Fenchurch Street) G4

Lloyds Avenue was built in the year 1894 when the south-eastern end of Fenchurch Street was reconstructed. The street was named after the buildings of Lloyd's *Register of*

Shipping, which were erected on the corner of Fenchurch Street.

LOMBARD COURT EC4 (Gracechurch Street) F4
Named after the Italian Lombard bankers who occupied this area in the fourteenth century (see Lombard Street). In the middle of the sixteenth century an old house in Lombard Court was occupied by the Lord Mayor, Sir William Chester; this, Lombard House, was probably the property of one of the Lombard families.

LOMBARD LANE EC3 (Temple Lane) B3
The rogues and poor people of *Alsatia*, as the southern side of Fleet Street was known, were nearly always in debt to the moneylenders of the City, so much so that the whole street was said to belong to the Lombards, the City's largest money-lenders. The street was formerly Lombard Street but was later renamed Lombard Lane to avoid confusion.

LOMBARD STREET EC3 (Gracechurch Street) F4
When the Jews were expelled from this country in the late thirteenth century by Edward I their place as bankers and general financiers was taken by the *Longobards* or Lombards, who came here from northern Italy and settled in what is now called Lombard Street. The Lombards were the financial geniuses of Europe, and were often summoned to help European countries that were in financial difficulties. They formed an organisation called the Society of the Bardi, and dominated the world of moneylending, banking and dealing in jewels until the reign of Queen Elizabeth I, when English merchants had learnt the art of banking sufficiently well to fend for themselves.

Lombard Street was destroyed in the Great Fire of 1666 and was completely rebuilt at a later date. Sir Robert Vyner, Lord Mayor of London in 1674, and the head of the great banking family of Goldsmiths, built his mansion on the site of what is now Post Office Court, which runs off Lombard Street. In 1705 the mansion was converted into the City's first General Post Office.

On the corner of Abchurch Lane a plaque marks the site of Edward Lloyd's coffee house which stood here from 1691 until 1785. In 1726 Lloyd's published what was probably one of the world's first newspapers, *Lloyd's List*.

On the northern side of the street stands the church of St Edmund the King which has stood on this site since Saxon times, when it was dedicated to King Edmund. The present church was built by Sir Christopher Wren to replace the one destroyed in the Great Fire.

At the north-eastern end of Lombard Street, on the site now occupied by the newly built Barclays Bank building, stood another of Wren's churches, called All Hallows, Lombard Street, which he rebuilt in 1694 to replace the original church destroyed in the Fire of 1666. The church was sold in 1938 to make way for an office block. That end of the street was rebuilt after the bombing of 1941.

LONDON BRIDGE EC4 (King William Street) F5

It is uncertain when the first bridge was built across the Thames, but Roman coins found in the middle of the river bed when the old wooden London bridge was demolished in 1831 suggest that one existed in Roman times. The first recorded bridge was built in the year 994, and in 1008 that bridge was defended by the Saxon King Ethelred, aided by his ally King Olave of Norway, against the attacking Danes. In 1176 a great new bridge was erected by Peter of Colechurch, a priest in the church of St Mary's which stood in Old Jewry. Peter of Colechurch built his bridge of wood, 180 ft east of the present London bridge in line with Fish Street Hill. In the middle of the bridge he erected a chapel to Thomas à Becket, and Peter of Colechurch himself was buried in the chapel in 1205. Houses were also built on the bridge and it became a fashionable place to live.

Gates were erected at both ends, the southern one being known as Traitors' Gate, because the heads of people executed for treason were displayed there; in 1305 the head of William Wallace, the brave Scot captured by Edward I, was displayed here after he had been hung, drawn and quartered at Smithfield. Here also were shown the heads of Archbishop Fisher and Sir Thomas More in 1535, after they had provoked the wrath of King Henry VIII.

The bridge, being constructed of wood, often caught fire and many of the houses built on it suffered the same fate. In the reign of Queen Elizabeth I the bridge ,and many fine new houses, were rebuilt; the largest of these was Nonsuch House, probably erected as a Lord Mayor's residence. In 1582 Peter Morris, a Dutchman, built a waterwheel at the northern end of the bridge to pump water to the City. Until the year 1750, when Westminster Bridge was constructed, London Bridge was the only bridge spanning the river and had, therefore, more than done its duty over the years. Towards the end of the eighteenth century it showed signs of collapsing, and in 1825 the building of a great new bridge, 180 ft west of the original, began, from a design by James Rennie. The bridge was completed in 1831 and was opened by King William IV and Queen Adelaide. A new approach road named King William Street was also constructed in honour of the reigning monarch, and the southern end of Gracechurch Street was altered to sweep westwards, away from Fish Street Hill, to meet the new bridge. Fish Street Hill, which served for 650 years as the approach road to the original bridge, was left in isolation, and today is used mainly by the porters of Billingsgate Market.

In 1921, during excavations for the removal of the Pearl Assurance buildings to Holborn, a complete arch of old London Bridge was discovered, and still remains below ground. The bridge of James Rennie is being dismantled to be shipped to the USA, to be re-erected as a tourist attraction at Lake Havasu, Arizona. A great new bridge is under construction, huge steel girders being moved into place.

LONDON'S BRIDGES F5, B4, D4, H5

Three bridges now span the River Thames within the City of London boundary—London Bridge, Blackfriars Bridge and Southwark Bridge. Blackfriars Bridge (see page 25) was built between 1760 and 1769; Southwark Bridge, constructed between 1815 and 1819 and designed by John Rennie, was built of iron and at first was called the Iron Bridge; it was considerably altered in 1919.

Tower Bridge was built in 1894 and designed by John Wolfe Barry. It lies outside the City boundary and is often confused by visitors with London Bridge.

LONDON STREET EC3 (Fenchurch Street) G4

John London was warden of the Ironmongers Company in 1724. The Ironmongers Hall stood in Fenchurch Street, almost opposite London Street, the first Hall being built in 1457. The hall was destroyed by enemy bombs in 1917 and a new one was built in Aldersgate Street in 1925.

LONDON WALL EC2 D2

London Wall follows the northern line of the old Roman wall. The Romans fortified *Londinium* by building a defensive wall from a point in the Tower of London in the east to Blackfriars in the west. The original thoroughfare called London Wall ran from Old Broad Street, taking a westerly course, to Wood Street, but the complete devastation of the area at the western end of London Wall during World War II gave the City corporation the opportunity to rebuild that end of the street and carry it right through to Aldersgate Street. The corporation intended calling this new thoroughfare Route 11, it being the eleventh proposition in the City of London improvement scheme, but the name of London Wall was eventually retained after strong protests from people keen on keeping the old City street names.

At the eastern end of the street, on the northern side, is the church of All Hallows in the Wall, built in 1765–7 by George Dance to replace the original fifteenth-century church. A portion of the Roman wall can be seen in the churchyard of All Hallows. A little farther west on the corner of Throgmorton Avenue stands the newly built hall of the Carpenters Company (see Throgmorton Avenue). On the northern side of the street a plaque on London Wall Buildings marks the site of the second Bethlehem, or Bedlam Hospital for the insane. The hospital originally stood on the site occupied by Liverpool Street station but was removed to London Wall in 1676, where it stood until 1815 when it was again removed, this time to Kennington.

The western end of the street has been completely rebuilt, and huge office blocks have been erected on both sides of it. On the northern side is the ruin of the church of St Alphage, which was built in 1777 on the site of the chapel of a fourteenth-century church, St Mary the Virgin. Behind the ruin of St Alphage the street now named St Alphage Gardens is really the only remaining portion of the original London Wall Street, and shows clearly how the new London Wall was redirected. In the old London Wall (now St Alphage Gardens) stood the hospital called Elsynge Spital, founded in 1331 by William Elsynge for the blind people of the City. The hospital fell into disuse and in 1630 Sion College was built on the site; the college was founded as a rest home for the City clergy and a place where they could study theology. The college was removed in 1886 to the Victoria Embankment where it still stands today.

The Curriers Hall, the home of the centuries-old trade of the curriers or tanners of leather, stood on the southern side of old London Wall. This building disappeared when the first bomb fell on the City of London in 1940.

The actual course of the old Roman wall lies some 15 ft

Page 125 The Stocks Market, site of the Mansion House

Page 126 The Mansion House in 1750 and today

below the modern City of London, and many of the streets follow its line. On the eastern side the wall commences near the White Tower in the Tower of London, and heads northwards, just to the east of Coopers Row, where, in the courtyard of Midland House, the best piece of wall can be seen. There is also a section to be seen just south of Midland House in Trinity Place. The wall continues northwards, forming part of the foundations of number 1 Crutched Friars, and runs through the foundations of buildings on the eastern side of Jewry Street to the junction of Aldgate, where the main gate called Aldgate spanned the road between Jewry Street and Dukes Place. The wall then veers to the northwest along the eastern side of Dukes Place, Bevis Marks, and Camomile Street, and sections of it have been found on several occasions whenever rebuilding has taken place in these streets. At the junction of Camomile Street and Wormwood Street stood the Bishop's Gate, and a plaque on the wall of Messrs Horne Bros marks the site of the gate.

The wall then runs almost due west along the northern side of the street called London Wall, and at the junction of Moorgate stood the northern entrance called Moor Gate. From here the wall turns slightly north-west to run between Fore Street and St Alphage Gardens. A plaque on the newly constructed Roman House marks the position of the City's other northern entrance, Cripple Gate, which spanned Wood Street. On the western side of Wood Street, beyond the new Monkwell Square, can be seen some of the bastions of the western section of the wall; it was in this area, after the bombing had flattened everything, that the City's archaeologists discovered the outline of a Roman fort which must have occupied the whole of the area from St Giles' church to St Anne's and St Agnes' church in Noble Street, across and slightly north of Gresham Street to Aldermanbury and back up to St Alphage Gardens. The Roman wall follows the line of the western wall of the fort by crossing the new London Wall to Noble Street; at the corner of London

Wall and Noble Street another good piece of it can be seen.

From this section in Noble Street the wall turns westwards just before St Anne's and St Agnes' church, to cross Aldersgate Street, where stood Alders Gate. The wall continues westwards through the foundations of the GPO buildings, where another section above ground can be seen by written request to the General Post Office. From this section the wall turns south to cross Newgate Street, where stood the western entrance called New Gate, running in line with the eastern side of Old Bailey—where excavations for the extension of the Central Criminal Court have revealed further sections of wall. At the southern end of Old Bailey, between it and the church of St Martin, stood the gate of old King Lud, called Lud Gate. The wall then runs westwards again, in line with Pilgrim Street, and strikes south to the river, running parallel with New Bridge Street.

The seven main gates of the City all stood until 1760, when they were pulled down, the stones being used to support the decaying old London Bridge. Until the early twelfth century a wall also enclosed the southern end of the City, running along what are now Upper and Lower Thames Streets; this wall had two gates, Dow Gate and Billings Gate. The southern wall was eventually demolished to give better access to the river.

LONG LANE EC1 (Aldersgate Street) D1
Long Lane is so named because it formed the long northern boundary of the old St Bartholomew Priory, which was founded in 1123 and dissolved in 1539 by Henry VIII. In the seventeenth century Long Lane was famous for its second-hand dealers, who sold mainly old linen, and also for its pawnbrokers and moneylenders.

LOTHBURY EC2 (Princes Street) E3
A family named Loteringi is recorded as living in this street in the early twelfth century, and the name of the street is said

128

to be a corruption of Loteringi Bury. It was first shortened to Loter Bury and eventually became known as Lothbury.

Another explanation sometimes offered is that the street was given its name because of the loathsome noise of the iron-founders who worked in what is now called Founders Court, an alleyway on the north side of Lothbury.

On the northern side is the church of St Margaret Loth-bury, rebuilt by Sir Christopher Wren to replace a thirteenth-century church destroyed in the Fire of 1666.

LOVAT LANE EC3 (Eastcheap) F4
The lane is named after Simon Fraser, Lord Lovat, who has the dubious distinction of being the last man to be beheaded in England. He was executed in 1747 on nearby Tower Hill for his part in the Jacobite rising of 1745.

LOVE LANE EC2 (Aldermanbury) D2
In the Middle Ages the wanton women of the City gathered in this lane, seeking customers, and the street thereby acquired its name. On the corner of Love Lane and Aldermanbury stood the church of St Mary Aldermanbury, which was damaged by German bombs in 1940, and was later shipped stone by stone to America, where it has been erected at Fulton, Missouri to the original specifications of Sir Christopher Wren, who rebuilt the church after the Great Fire. The old churchyard of St Mary has been converted into a small garden, which contains a memorial to Henry Condell and John Heminge, the actor friends of William Shakespeare who collected together his works and gave them to the world in 1623. Both these men were buried in the old church of St Mary Aldermanbury.

LOWER THAMES STREET EC3 (London Bridge) F5
Called 'Lower' Thames Street because it lay below old London Bridge, the street has for centuries been the home of those who have traded on the river.

At the western end, near London Bridge, stands the old church of St Magnus the Martyr, which was first built in 1302 at the northern end of old London Bridge (see London Bridge). In that church was buried Miles Coverdale, who wrote the first complete English translation of the Bible. The church was one of the first buildings to be consumed by the Great Fire of London, which started almost opposite in Pudding Lane. Sir Christopher Wren rebuilt the church between 1671 and 1687.

The area of the church is taken up by the great fish market called Billingsgate, which is said to take its name from King Belin who erected a water gate on this site 400 years before the birth of Christ. Billingsgate became a fish market over 600 years ago when it was moved to this site from the old market near Friday Street. Billingsgate market was completely rebuilt in the middle of the nineteenth century, but the method of selling fish has hardly changed from early times. The hustle and bustle of the market can best be seen in the early hours of the morning, and a sight to watch for is that of a market porter nonchalantly carrying a dozen fish baskets on his head.

Opposite Billingsgate market there stood, until recently, the great Coal Exchange, which was built in 1849 but damaged in the bombing of 1941 and recently demolished. The two statues of dragons holding the shield of the City of London were saved when the building was demolished, and they now stand on the Victoria Embankment, marking the extreme western boundary of the City.

At the eastern end of Lower Thames Street stands the Custom House, the headquarters of the Customs and Excise. A custom house was first erected on this site by John Churchman, Sheriff of London in 1385. A much larger building was erected in the sixteenth century to cope with the increase in imports, but it was destroyed in the Fire of 1666, and an even larger building, designed by Sir Christopher Wren, was also destroyed by a fire, in 1715. Another building was erected between 1814 and 1817 and this too was nearly destroyed, this time by German bombs in 1941. The Custom House has been completely restored, and now occupies the whole of the south-eastern end of the street. The northern side of that end suffered badly during the bombing, but it has all been completely rebuilt. The Tiger tavern, now built into the huge office block erected on the northern side of the street, replaces a tavern of that name which once stood on Tower Hill and was honoured by a visit from Queen Elizabeth I in 1558, when she was on her way to Tilbury to inspect the troops awaiting the arrival of the Spanish Armada.

LUDGATE BROADWAY EC4 (Pilgrim Street) C3
Originally this street was known just as The Broadway; it was the widest thoroughfare in this area of little narrow lanes running off Ludgate Hill.

LUDGATE CIRCUS EC4 (Fleet Street) B3
Built in 1875 the Circus stands on the site of the Fleet Bridge which connected Ludgate Hill with Fleet Street in the days when the Fleet river flowed where Farrington Street and New Bridge Street now stand. Part of the wooden supports of that bridge have been found from time to time during excavations.

On the south-eastern side of the Circus, between what is now a restaurant and a theatre booking-office kiosk, is a plaque marking the site of the offices of the *Daily Courant*, which was published in 1702 and was acclaimed as Britain's first daily newspaper.

On the north-eastern corner, on the wall of a bank, is a memorial tablet to Edgar Wallace, the author, who started his career as a Fleet Street journalist.

LUDGATE HILL EC4 (Ludgate Circus) C3
Ludgate Hill is one of the two hills upon which the City of London is built. The thoroughfare formerly led to the City

131

gate called Lud Gate, the site of which is marked by a plaque on the side of St Martin's church. The old gate is said to have been named after King Lud who, in 66 BC, built an entrance to the City on this site and who was eventually buried there.

One of the most criticized structures in the nineteenth century was the viaduct which the London, Chatham & Dover Railway Company erected to carry its trains over Ludgate Hill. That viaduct survived the bombing of London and still stands today, blocking the view of St Paul's from Fleet Street. Recent building near St Paul's has now practically hidden all but the dome from anyone walking up Ludgate Hill.

Before the end of this street was obliterated by German bombs in 1940, there stood, between the viaduct and Old Bailey, the Bell Sauvage Yard, which was the entrance to the famous old fifteenth-century hostelry called La Belle Sauvage. The inn was one of the City's most famous coaching inns and people gathered daily to watch the coaches leave the yard and clatter up Ludgate Hill. It was demolished in 1873, and Hillgate House now occupies its site. On the nothern side stands the church of St Martin within Ludgate, which dates back to the seventh century. The church was rebuilt in 1437 but destroyed in the Fire of 1666; Sir Christopher Wren rebuilt the present church in 1687. The western side of the church was close to the old City wall, and a plaque on that side marks the position of the Lud Gate, demolished in 1760.

A statue of Queen Elizabeth I, erected when the gate was rebuilt during her reign, was saved when the gate was eventually demolished, and was erected on the eastern side of St Dunstan-in-the-West in Fleet Street, where it can still be seen.

A little of the old City wall can be seen at the rear of St Martin's church in Amen Court.

MAGPIE ALLEY EC4 (Whitefriars Street) B3
Named in memory of an inn called the Magpie, one of the

many taverns in this area. The alley forms a little entrance to the buildings of the *Daily Mail*.

MAIDENHEAD COURT EC1 (Aldersgate Street) D2
A tavern called the Mayden Heade stood near this court-way, which was then known as Lamb's Court. John Milton lived in Lamb's Court in 1645 and started his writing career there.

MANSELL STREET E1 (Algate High Street) H3
In the seventeenth century, when the land east of Aldgate was still farmland and open fields, there took place in the church of St Dunstan-in-the-East near Eastcheap a marriage between Mansell Leman and Lucy Alie. The families of the young couple were rich local landowners, and were of sufficient importance to have the new streets built in that area named after them. Only the northern end of Mansell Street lies within the City boundary, but outside the boundary lie the streets called Leman Street and Alie Street.

MANSION HOUSE PLACE EC4 (East of the Mansion House) E3
Mansion House Place was formerly George Street and forms an entrance to the Mansion House from St Swithins Lane.

MANSION HOUSE STREET EC3 (Poultry) E3
In the middle of the eighteenth century, when the building of the residence of the Lord Mayor of London was completed, the roadway in front of it, ie the eastern section of Poultry, was renamed Mansion House Street.

The idea of an official residence for the City's Lord Mayor had long been in the minds of the City corporation, and in 1728 a committee was set up to determine the cost and to select a suitable site. The site selected was that of the ancient Stocks Market, which dated back to the thirteenth century. The market was built on the site of the old City stocks, hence

its name, and sold mainly fish; it was destroyed in the Great
Fire of 1666 and when it was rebuilt it became a flower and
vegetable market.

Near the old marketplace was the thirteenth-century
St Mary Woolchurch, and in the churchyard stood the beam
used for the official weighing of wool. The church perished
in the flames of the Great Fire and was not rebuilt, only a
small portion of the graveyard remaining.

In the market stood a statue of Charles II on horse-
back, which had been presented to the Corporation by Sir
Robert Vyner, Lord Mayor in 1673. In 1738 work started
on the clearing of the site, the ancient market and the graveyard of St Mary Woolchurch were demolished, and the
statue of King Charles II was returned to the Vyner family;
it stands to this day in the grounds of their home at Newby
Hall in Yorkshire.

In 1739 the foundation stone of the Mansion House was
laid, but it was not until 1753 that the current Lord Mayor,
Sir Crisp Gascoigne, was able to take up residence. The
house became one of the sights of the City and crowds
gathered to see it; the more fortunate were allowed to inspect
the inside of the mansion, and to see the Egyptian Hall, the
banqueting room where nearly 400 guests can be entertained.
The Mansion House was damaged by enemy action in 1940
but has been completely restored, and plaques on the western
wall remember the old Stocks Market and the church of St
Mary Woolchurch.

MARK LANE EC3 (Great Tower Street) G4

According to John Stow's sixteenth-century *Survey of London*,
the north-eastern corner of Mark Lane was taken up, in the
fourteenth century, by the manor house and grounds of Sir
Thomas Ross, a knight of King Richard II. The manor,
Blanche Appleton, was granted by Edward IV a hundred
years later to the basketmakers, as a marketplace where they
could *mart*, or sell their wares. The lane leading to the market

was called Mart Lane, of which the present name is a corruption. Blanche Appleton was remembered by a little courtway called Blind Chapel Court, but that courtway and the last memory of Blanche Appleton disappeared when the area was reconstructed during the nineteenth century.

At the south-eastern side of Mark Lane stands the Corn Exchange Buildings, first opened in 1747, but rebuilt and enlarged in 1881 owing to the increase in trade. The Exchange was especially busy on a Monday when dealers in corn, wheat, maize, barley, and all forms of modern cereals flocked there to do business. Cereal House is a more modern extension to the Corn Exchange. Opposite the Exchange are the huge buildings called King Beam House, the offices of HM Customs and Excise.

At the north-western end, by Star Alley, is the tower of the early fourteenth-century church of All Hallows Staining, so named because it was one of the first churches to be built of stone, or *stane*, all early churches normally being built of wood. It escaped the Great Fire but fell down in 1671, was rebuilt in 1675 and lasted until it was demolished (all but the tower) in 1870 by the Clothworkers Company, which purchased the land in order to extend its premises. Its tower was saved in order that the memory of one of the City's earliest stone churches should remain, and although the Clothworkers Hall, in Mincing Lane, was destroyed in the bombing, it still survives.

MARTIN LANE EC4 (Cannon Street) F4

A medieval church called St Martin Orgar stood on the eastern side of the lane, but it was destroyed in the Great Fire of 1666 and lay in ruins until 1820, when it was completely demolished to make way for office blocks. The architects retained the memory of old St Martin Orgar by rebuilding the medieval tower and incorporating it into the office building. The tower can best be seen from Cannon Street, and is easily distinguished by its old overhanging clock.

MASONS AVENUE EC2 (Basinghall Street) E3

The Masons Hall stood on this site. The Masons naturally played a big part in the rebuilding of the City after the Great Fire of 1666, but their Hall was demolished when the area was destroyed in 1941.

In modern Masons Avenue stands the popular City tavern called Ye Olde Dr Butlers Head. Doctor William Butler, physician to James I, invented a medicated ale which, he claimed, rejuvenated all who drank it. Dr Butler set up a number of taverns in the City, and the present one in Masons Avenue, though badly bombed, has been restored, and is once again a popular tavern.

MIDDLE STREET EC1 (Cloth Street) C1

When the great St Batholomew priory, which occupied the whole of this area, was dissolved in 1539, the monastic building and land were granted to Sir Richard Rich, whose family held the land until the early nineteenth century. During the seventeenth century the family erected many houses and streets. Middle Street was simply the street built between two older streets, East Passage and Newbury Street.

MIDDLE TEMPLE LANE EC4 (Fleet Street) A3

In Fleet Street, opposite Temple Bar, stands the old Middle Temple Gate, built from a design by Sir Christopher Wren in 1684. The Middle Temple boasts such famous students as Edmund Plowden, a great judge during the reign of Elizabeth I; Inigo Jones, the seventeenth-century architect; Charles Dickens; and John Evelyn, the diarist, who with Samuel Pepys recorded the Great Fire of London. Also students in the Middle Temple were many men who were to become famous lawyers in the American colonies; five of them, Edward Routledge, Thomas Heyward, Thomas McKean, Thomas Lynch, and Arthur Middleton were to become even better known by putting their signatures to the Declaration of Independence on 4 July 1776.

136

A walk down the Middle Temple Lane leads past Brick Court where Oliver Goldsmith lodged and died in 1774. Brick Court was destroyed in the bombing, but has since been rebuilt. Opposite are the seventeenth-century buildings called Pump Court to which Charles Dickens often referred in *Martin Chuzzlewit*. A little farther down the lane lies the famous Temple Fountain, and beyond that the Middle Temple Hall, which was built about 1573. Although damaged by bombs in the last war it has been restored and is one of the finest examples of Elizabethan craftsmanship in London. The arms and banners of the famous people who have been entertained there were removed to safety before the bombing started, and have since been returned to the Hall. In 1601, on a dais at the western end of the Hall, Shakespeare presented his first performance of *Twelfth Night* in the presence of Queen Elizabeth I. That same queen gave the Middle Temple the huge oak table that stands on the dais, and at which successful candidates are 'called to the Bar'. Beyond the Hall the Middle Temple Gardens stretch to the Victoria Embankment, and during the lunch hour famous barristers and lawyers can be seen strolling with clients.

MIDDLESEX PASSAGE EC1 (Bartholomew Close) C2

A very large sixteenth-century house called Middlesex House stood here, and the passageway is named after it.

MIDDLESEX STREET E1 (Bishopsgate to Aldgate High Street) G2

In the fourteenth century the street was a country lane called Berwardes Lane, after a landowner of that name. In the sixteenth century the name was changed to Hog Lane, because its course ran through the many pig farms that had sprung up in the area, and John Stow in his *Survey of London*, which was first published in 1598, says:

this Hog Lane stretcheth north towards St Mary Spitle without Bishopsgate, and within these fortie-four years last had on both sides fair hedge rows of elm trees with bridges and easy stiles to pass over into the pleasant fields very commodious for citizens therein to walk, shoot and otherwise recreate and refresh their dull spirits in the sweet and wholesome air.

In the seventeenth century the pleasant Hog Lane became the haunt of Jewish secondhand-clothes dealers and was renamed Pettycoatlane. By the nineteenth century it was no longer a pleasant country lane and was given the unimaginative name of Middlesex Street, after the county near which it lies. Despite its renaming, Middlesex Street has for the last 100 years been London's premier Sunday-morning market to which thousands flock looking for bargains, and it is still known affectionately as Petticoat Lane; many people, even Londoners, do not know that its real name is Middlesex Street.

MILES LANE EC4 (Arthur Street) F4

A fourteenth-century church called St Michael Crooked Lane stood on the eastern side of Miles Lane (a corruption of St Michaels Lane) at the junction of a street called Crooked Lane. The church was erected about 1367 by John Lovekyn, the Lord Mayor and a member of the Fishmongers Company. Another famous Fishmonger, Sir William Walworth, built a college at the side of the church, and was buried in the church in 1385. The church and the college were destroyed in the Great Fire of 1666, and the church was rebuilt by Sir Christopher Wren.

In 1831, when the new London Bridge was constructed, Crooked Lane (so called because it took a crooked course between Miles Lane and Fish Street Hill), the northern end of Miles Lane, and the church of St Michael were all demolished to make way for the new approach road, King William Street.

MILK STREET EC2 (Cheapside) D3

In medieval times the people of the City purchased their milk from this tributary of the great Cheapside market.

In Milk Street, in 1480, was born London's famous six-teenth-century chancellor, Sir Thomas More. He was edu-cated in a school in Threadneedle Street, then passed on to Oxford to study law; he later became one of England's most eminent lawyers, and a great friend of Henry VIII. That friendship ended when Sir Thomas More opposed Henry's petition for divorce from his first wife, Katharine of Aragon, and when Henry's marriage to Anne Boleyn was announced Sir Thomas resigned his chancellorship. Henry VIII was furious, and charged him with treason, committing him to the Tower of London. He was tried, and executed on Tower Hill, in 1535.

There stood in Milk Street, before it was burnt down by the Great Fire of 1666, the tiny parish church of St Mary Magdalen. The church was not rebuilt, and the parish was united with that of the adjacent St Lawrence Jewry.

In 1837 the City of London School was erected in Milk Street with money bequeathed for the purpose by John Car-penter, the City Clerk in the reign of Henry V. The school was removed to its present site on the Victoria Embankment in 1882.

On 29 December 1940 much of the area was destroyed by bombs, necessitating the rebuilding of many streets, including Milk Street.

MILTON STREET EC2 (Chiswell Street) E1

The street was formerly called Grub Street and was renamed in 1830 in memory of John Milton, the poet.

In the fifteenth century it was occupied by bowyers and fletchers (arrowmakers), who supplied the needs of the archers that practised daily on the moor fields just to the north of the City Wall. By the eighteenth century the street had been taken over by authors and poets of no reputation, and any poor publication of that era was said to be a product of Grub Street.

In the sevententh century one of the City's most famous

characters was Henry Welby, the Grub Street hermit. Welby, a wealthy and educated man, lived in three rooms of a house in Grub Street for forty years without venturing outside, the only person to see him being a female servant who attended him. Welby died in 1636 aged eighty-four and when his body, with its long locks of hair and huge beard, was carried for burial to St Giles Cripplegate folk said that it was the first time for forty years that it had seen the light of day.

In Sweedons Passage, which with the rest of this area was obliterated by the first bombs to fall on the City in 1940, there stood until as late as 1850 a very large old crumbling mansion which was said to have been the home of Richard Whittington, and much later the home of Sir Thomas Gresham.

Only the northern end of Milton Street survived the bombing of 1940; the southern end, which extended to Fore Street, is still part of the wilderness of the devastated Barbican area, upon which modern multi-storey flats and office blocks are springing up like mushrooms.

MINCING LANE EC3 (Fenchurch Street) G4

Minchun, the medieval name for a female monk or nun, was the original name of the lane given because the houses in the lane were owned by the nuns, or *minchuns*, of St Helen's Priory in Bishopsgate. Since 1456 the north-eastern end of Mincing Lane has been occupied by the successive Halls of the Clothworkers Company, the twelfth of the twelve great City livery companies. The largest of the Clothworkers Halls was built in 1860 but it was completely destroyed in the bombing of World War II. The Clothworkers Hall is now situated in Dunster Court, and a huge office block has been erected since the war on the site of the bombed Hall. The Clothworkers emblem, the ram, can be seen above the iron gates of Dunster Court.

The western side of Mincing Lane is taken up by Plantation House, the headquarters of tea dealers, and also the home of the Rubber Exchange.

MINORIES EC3 (Aldgate High Street) H3
In 1293, on the site now occupied by St Clare House, Edmund, Earl of Lancaster and brother of Edward I, founded an abbey for Spanish nuns, which was dedicated to St Clare; the nuns were called *Sorores Minores* or 'little sisters of St Clare'. The abbey was dissolved by Henry VIII and passed to the Bishop of Bath and Wells, who converted the building into a private residence; only the church of the nunnery, Holy Trinity Minories, was left standing. In 1552 the property was given to the Duke of Suffolk by Edward VI, but the Duke did not hold it for long: in 1554 he was beheaded on Tower Hill. Holy Trinity church was completely rebuilt in 1706, and was in use until 1899 when it was converted into a parish room for St Botolph's Aldgate. In 1851, during work carried out on the vaults of the old church, a human head, preserved in a sawdust barrel, was uncovered; the head is almost certainly that of the executed former owner of the property, the Duke of Suffolk. For years the head was exhibited in Holy Trinity church for all to see, but since the church was annexed to St Botolph's the head has been preserved there, and can only be seen by application. Holy Trinity church was destroyed by German bombs, and the modern office block called St Clare House has been erected on the site.

MITRE COURT EC2 (Milk Street) D3
The court is named in memory of the famous fifteenth-century Mitre Tavern, which stood on the corner of Bread Street and Cheapside, and was constantly mentioned in plays and books of the sixteenth and seventeenth centuries. The tavern was completely destroyed in the Great Fire of 1666 and the site is now occupied by a modern office block.

MITRE STREET EC3 (Aldgate) G3

In the sixteenth century a tavern called the Mitre was built here in memory of the Priory of Holy Trinity which was founded by Queen Matilda, the wife of Henry I, in 1108 and occupied the whole of this area. The priory was dissolved in 1539 and the property eventually passed to the Duke of Norfolk, who is remembered in nearby Dukes Place.

In 1622, in what is now Mitre Square, a small church was built and called Trinity Christchurch, but later renamed St James in honour of James I. The church was demolished in 1874 and the Corporation has remembered both the old priory and St James Church by setting plaques in the walls of buildings in Mitre Square.

Mitre Street became famous for a more sinister reason; for in 1869 one of the victims of Jack the Ripper was found in the gutter, and for months afterwards the street was full of morbidly inquisitive sightseers.

The street was badly hit by bombs in World War II, and to this day the destruction is still evident at the southern end.

MONKWELL SQUARE EC2 (Wood Street) D2

Monkwell Square is a modern square erected upon the site of Monkwell Street and Hart Street, both obliterated by German bombs in 1940. Monkwell Street (Monks Well Street) stood on the site of a well owned by the Abbot of Garendon and used by the monks. In the thirteenth century a family called Munchewella is recorded as living in Mukewellstrate, and the family probably took their name from the old monks' well. Until 1874 the chapel of St James in the Wall stood in Monkwell Street, a relic of the ancient Abbey of Garendon. The most famous building in the street was the Hall of the Barbers Company, which was built in 1636 by Inigo Jones to replace the original mid-fifteenth century Hall. In 1540 the Barbers were united with the Guild of Surgeons, and a picture by Hans Holbein, depicting Henry VIII performing this ceremony, graced the Hall for over 300

Page 143 (*above*) The Royal Exchange; (*below*) the statue of Mary Queen of Scots in Fleet Street, next door to the Cheshire Cheese

Page 144 (above) The Palace of Bridewell in the seventeenth century, showing the section of the River Fleet now covered by New Bridge Street; (below) Farringdon Street, the site of the River Fleet, stretching away to Clerkenwell

years; it was removed to safety with many of the Company's treasures, before the commencement of the bombing of 1940, and will grace the fine new Hall that is nearing completion on the western side of Monkwell Square. Behind the Barbers Hall the City Corporation has cleared the rubble left after the bombing, and portions of the bastions of the old City wall can clearly be seen.

MONTAGUE COURT EC1 (Little Britain) C2

The mansion of Lord Montague occupied the whole of this side of Little Britain in the sixteenth century, and the court was named after the household.

MONUMENT STREET EC3 (King William Street) F4

In 1887 a new thoroughfare was constructed from Billings-gate Market to King William Street to enable market traffic to reach London Bridge easily, and the thoroughfare, be-cause it passed Wren's monument to the Great Fire of London, was called Monument Street.

A little to the east of Fish Street Hill, in the middle of Monument Street, rises the Monument—erected from a de-sign by Sir Christopher Wren and completed in 1670 at a cost of £13,450 11s 9d. It stands on the site of the churchyard of St Margarets Fish Street Hill which perished in the flames of the Great Fire, and rises 202 ft high, that being the exact distance from the pedestal to the site in Pudding Lane where the Fire began.

The Fire started at 2 am on Sunday, 2 September 1666 in the house of William Farryner, the King's baker, in Pudding Lane. No one knows who started it, but for many years it was attributed to Catholics, and until 1830 the inscription on the northern panel of the Monument included the words: '. . . but Popish frenzy, which wrought such horror, is not yet quenched'. The flames, fanned by an easterly wind, quickly spread through the City, consuming 89 churches, 13,200 houses, and 400 streets, and were not arrested until

Thursday, 6 September. A committee set up to inquire into the cause of the fire gave the verdict that it was an Act of God, a great easterly wind and a very dry season.

The Monument was fortunate in escaping the bombing of London. It was cleaned in 1954 to remove bomb scars, and at the same time the gilt bronze urn at the top of the column was regilded. Six people have committed suicide by jumping from the public gallery, and since the last death, in 1842, this has been caged in.

MOOR HOUSE PODIUM EC2 E2
The newly constructed Moor House was the first new building erected on the bomb-ravaged area to incorporate a podium, or elevated footway, which separates pedestrians from the traffic using London Wall.

MOOR LANE EC2 E2
Before the construction of the first Moor Gate in 1415, Moor Lane was, as the name suggests, a narrow lane leading from near the Cripple Gate to the open moorlands north of the City wall.

Moor Lane was one of the few thoroughfares in this area to survive the bombing well enough to be rebuilt, and twenty-five years after the end of the war the rebuilding is nearing completion; when the huge office blocks are finished the lane will hardly recall a narrow path leading out to marshy countryside.

MOORFIELDS EC2 (Moor Place to Moorgate) E2
Formerly called Little Moorfields, the street name perpetuates the days before the seventeenth century when the whole of the area north of London Wall was open land.

In 1415 Thomas Falconer, the Lord Mayor, ordered a postern gate to be erected, which he called the Moor Gate, to enable the people of the City to reach the countryside more easily. In the summer women took their washing out to the Moorfields to dry, and children used it as their play-ground. The City's trained bands practised archery there, and about 1620 they built a permanent barracks in the fields; it was to be the forerunner of the present Honourable Artillery Company grounds in City Road.

In 1666, after the Great Fire, the fields were used to house the thousands made homeless and Bunhill Cemetery is said to be the bone-hill where thousands of victims of the plague of 1665 and the Great Fire were buried. In the late seventeenth century the land was drained, and the present streets were completed by the beginning of the nineteenth century.

MOORGATE EC2 (Finsbury Pavement to Princes Street) E2

The thoroughfare called Moorgate was created in 1846 to ease the traffic problem in this area, and was designed to run from the site of the old Moor Gate, from which it takes its name, to the Bank of England. Before its construction north-to-south traffic used mainly the narrow Coleman Street.

The first gate was cut into the northern section of the old City wall in 1415 to give access to the open moorland which lay north of the wall, and this postern gate was later enlarged to become one of the seven main gates to the City. By the middle of the eighteenth century the old City wall had crumbled beyond use and the gates were no longer necessary; in 1760 they were all demolished, the stones of the Moor Gate being used to support the decaying London Bridge. A plaque on 75 Moorgate marks the site of the old gate.

Just to the north of the site of the Moor Gate stands the City of London College. The original college was built in White Street, just south of Ropemaker Street in 1883, but street and college were blasted out of existence by German bombs in 1940, and the college was later rebuilt on its present site.

MUSCOVY STREET EC3 (Trinity Square) G4

Peter the Great, the founder of the Russian Empire, visited

147

this country in 1698 to learn the art of shipbuilding, and he was a frequent visitor to a tavern in Great Tower Street. The original name of that tavern is obscure, but Peter the Great was such a good customer that it was changed to The Czar of Muscovy. Muscovy Street was also named in his honour.

NEW BRIDGE STREET EC4 B3
In 1769 the new Blackfriars Bridge, or Pitt Bridge as it was then called, was opened, and the approach road to it was called New Bridge Street. The street was constructed between 1760 and 1768 and was built upon arches to cover the last remaining open stretch of the old Fleet River, which the City engineers had plans to convert into a sewer.

In the early sixteenth century the banks of this stretch of the River Fleet were occupied by two great buildings—on the eastern side the monastery of the Black Friars (see Blackfriars Lane), and on the western side by the Palace of Bridewell (see Bridewell Place).

NEW BROAD STREET EC2 F2
The street was constructed in 1737 on part of the site of the old Bethlehem Hospital (see Liverpool Street), and was named Petty France because of the many French people living in the vicinity. The City Corporation renamed the street in the nineteenth century when new office blocks were erected on both sides of it.

NEW CHANGE EC4 (Cannon Street) D3
When this area, just to the east of St Paul's cathedral, was hit by German bombs in 1940, among the many streets destroyed was an ancient thoroughfare called Old Change, which ran from Knightrider Street to Cheapside, just to the west of St Augustine's church. After the war, when the rubble was cleared, the City corporation cut a new and wider thoroughfare a little to the east of the original street and called it New Change (see Old Change Court).

NEW FETTER LANE EC4 (Holborn Circus) B2

When the area south of Holborn Circus was destroyed in 1941, one of the few streets to survive was a thoroughfare called Bartletts Buildings. Since the war Bartletts Buildings has been widened and extended to run in a westerly curve to join Fetter Lane, and the new thoroughfare was renamed New Fetter Lane. The whole of the western side of New Fetter Lane is taken up by the new *Daily Mirror* buildings, and the eastern side by large new office blocks.

NEW STREET HILL EC4 (Shoe Lane) B3

The area immediately north of Fleet Street, between Fetter Lane and Shoe Lane, was given to the Goldsmiths Company in 1513 by Agnes Harding. The Goldsmiths developed the area in the middle of the seventeenth century, naming two streets after their lady benefactor, East Harding Street and West Harding Street. The rest of the new streets were given the unimaginative names of New Street Hill, New Street Square, Great New Street and Little New Street.

NEWCASTLE CLOSE EC4 (Farringdon Street) B2

In the sixteenth century coal was carried in barges up the River Fleet and deposited near what is now called Sea Coal Lane. The sea-coal came from Newcastle, and Newcastle Close was probably named accordingly.

NEWCASTLE COURT EC4 (College Hill) E4

On this site stood the mansion of the Duke of Buckingham, destroyed in the Great Fire of 1666. The entrance to the Duke's house was called Castle Court after the castle or tower in which King Stephen lived in the twelfth century. The King's residence, the Tower Royal, stood opposite the northern end of College Hill in Cannon Street. When Castle Court was rebuilt in the nineteenth century it was renamed New Castle Court.

NEWGATE STREET EC1 (Holborn Viaduct) C3

A new gate was built into the western side of the City wall in the early twelfth century to replace the original Roman gate. It was erected across the old Roman road called Watling Street, and because of it that section of Watling Street was eventually renamed Newgate Street.

Towards the end of the twelfth century the gatehouse was used as a prison, and when the gate was rebuilt again in the early fifteenth century the Lord Mayor, Richard Whittington, gave money for the rebuilding and extending of the prison, which stood until 1902 when it was demolished to make way for the Central Criminal Courts (see Old Bailey). The New Gate was rebuilt after the Great Fire, but it was finally demolished in 1767.

In medieval times Newgate Street became the home of the City butchers, whose stalls occupied the whole of the centre of the street, and the middle section, where they were at their thickest, was known as The Shambles. The extreme western end of Newgate Street was for a time known as Blow Bladder Lane, because the butchers inserted sheep's bladders into the meat carcasses and inflated them, making the carcasses deceptively larger.

Two churches stood on opposite sides of The Shambles— on the northern side was St Nicholas Shambles, and almost opposite was the church of St Ewin—both were destroyed in the Great Fire of 1666. From the year 1306 the whole of the northern side of the street was occupied by the huge monastery of the Franciscans or Grey Friars. The monastery was dissolved by Henry VIII, who handed it to the City corporation. The old choir house was converted into a parish church and was called Christ Church. Henry's son, Edward VI, made good use of the Grey Friars property when he founded on the site a school for poor boys, Christ's Hospital. The church and the school were destroyed in the Great Fire of London. Wren rebuilt the Christ Church, the walls and tower of which can still be seen at the eastern end of Newgate

Street, the rest of the church having been removed by bombs in 1940. Christ's Hospital, or the Bluecoat school as it came to be called, was rebuilt and stood until 1902, when it was removed to Horsham in Sussex, and the GPO buildings were erected on its site.

One of the school's most famous pupils was Charles Lamb, who was a student there from 1782 until 1789; he immortalised the school when he wrote 'Recollections of Christ's Hospital' and 'Christ's Hospital Five and Thirty Years Ago'.

NEWMAN COURT EC3 (Cornhill) F3
The court is named in memory of Cardinal Newman, born in nearby Finch Lane in 1801. He was baptised in Wren's church of St Benet Fink, which was demolished in 1844 to make way for the building of the new Royal Exchange.

NICHOLAS LANE EC4 (Lombard Street) F4
A twelfth-century church called St Nicholas Acon stood on the western side of the lane, one of the eighty-nine churches destroyed in the Great Fire of London.

In 1850, during excavations at the southern end of Nicholas Lane, a Roman building was unearthed 10 ft below the ground.

NOBLE STREET EC2 (Gresham Street) D2
Thomas le Noble is recorded as being the owner of property in this street in the early fourteenth century, and the street was probably named after him.

Noble Street runs parallel with the western section of the old Roman wall, and formerly contained two churches, St Anne & St Agnes and, at the corner of Gresham Street, St John Zachary; both were destroyed in the Fire of 1666 and only St Anne & St Agnes was considered worth rebuilding. The church, sometimes called St Anne in the Willows, because of the willows that grew against the City wall, was rebuilt by Sir Christopher Wren in 1676–87, was destroyed again in 1940 by the first German bombs to fall on the City, and was completely rebuilt to the original Wren design by D. F. Martin-Smith in 1965. The bombs disclosed a portion of the old City wall, which can be seen on the western side, near the new thoroughfare called London Wall. At the corner of Gresham Street a tiny portion of the churchyard of St John Zachary can still be seen. The Hall of the Coach-makers Company, which stood on the eastern side of Noble Street, was also destroyed in the bombing.

Robert Tichborne, Lord Mayor of London in 1656, and one of the men who signed the death warrant of King Charles I, lived in Noble Street.

NORTHUMBERLAND ALLEY EC3 (Fenchurch Street) G4

On this site stood the fifteenth-century home of Henry Percy, the Earl of Northumberland. Northumberland House was vacated by the Percies in the late sixteenth century, and was eventually destroyed in the Great Fire of London.

OAT LANE EC2 (Noble Street) D2

The origin of the name of this lane seems to have been forgotten, but as it is situated quite near the old Cheapside market it seems probable that oats were sold there.

A church called St Mary Staining, which stood in Oat Lane, was destroyed in the Great Fire of London and was not rebuilt.

The Hall of the Pewterers Company has, since the war, been erected on the northern side of the lane, but it originally stood in Lime Street. The origin of the Pewterers can be traced back to the old tin mines of Cornwall.

OLD BAILEY EC4 (Ludgate Hill) C3

The origin of the name Old Bailey is uncertain, but the word *Bailey* means the outer wall of a feudal castle, or an extra line of fortification. The thoroughfare does, in fact, lie just to the west of the western section of the City wall, and in 1900 a portion of the old wall 8 ft high and 8 ft 3 in wide was found during the rebuilding of 7 and 8 Old Bailey.

On the site now occupied by the Central Criminal Court stood the infamous Newgate Prison; it was erected in the late twelfth century and was rebuilt on a number of occasions, the largest alteration taking place in the fifteenth century when Richard Whittington, the Lord Mayor of London, gave money to rebuild and extend it. Many relics of the old prison, such as whipping blocks, leg irons and thumbscrews can be seen in the Guildhall museum.

The prison was burnt down in the anti-Catholic riots led by Lord George Gordon in 1780. A new prison was erected on the same site and some of the first prisoners to be executed were the followers of Lord George; in 1793 he was executed himself for leading the riots. With the building of the new prison public hangings were transferred from Tyburn (Marble Arch), and from 1783 until 1868 crowds gathered regularly in Old Bailey to watch prisoners step on to the gallows. After 1868 hangings were carried out in private inside the prison. Until 1809 the Surgeons Hall stood, conveniently placed, next door to the prison so that executed prisoners could be immediately examined and dissected. In 1902 the old prison buildings were pulled down and the Central Criminal Court, nicknamed the Old Bailey, was erected on its site. The building was designed by E. W. Mountford, and was officially opened in 1907. One of the best-known sights in London is the copper-covered dome, surmounted by the figure of Justice.

Many famous people have lived in the thoroughfare called Old Bailey. At number 68 lived Jonathan Wild, one of London's most celebrated thieves; he used to receive stolen goods from his accomplices and then return them to their original owners for a consideration, but he was eventually caught, and was hung at Newgate on 24 May 1725.

The southern end of the Old Bailey suffered during the

bombing of 1941, and new office blocks have been erected on the western side.

OLD BROAD STREET EC2 (Threadneedle Street) F3
Old Broad Street was so called because it was one of the widest streets in the City.

Until the middle of the seventeenth century the street was also one of the most fashionable areas of the City. When the Augustinian priory was dissolved by Henry VIII (see Austin Friars), William Powlett, the Marquis of Winchester, built his house on the site which occupied most of the western side of the street. The new office block called Winchester House, rebuilt since the war, was named in memory of the Marquis, as is Great Winchester Street.

Almost next to the house of William Powlett stood a church called St Peter le Poor, dedicated to the poor people of the area. It was pulled down in 1792 and later rebuilt, but was eventually demolished in 1907 to make way for an office block.

Almost opposite the old site of St Peter le Poor, at number 19, stands the City of London Club, the meeting place of City bankers and merchants. Next door to the City of London Club, at number 24, a plaque marks the site of the house of Sir Thomas Gresham, founder of the Royal Exchange. Sir Thomas's house took up the whole of the area between Bishopsgate and Old Broad Street, and he lived there at intervals between 1563 and 1579. The office block now standing on the site is called Gresham House.

OLD CHANGE COURT EC4 (Carter Lane) C3
In the thirteenth century Old Change was a building where bullion was stored before being taken to the Mint to be coined.

Before the bombing of the area around St Paul's cathedral in 1941 Old Change ran between Knightrider Street and Cheapside, parallel with the eastern side of St Paul's churchyard. The street was completely destroyed but a large office block erected between Cannon Street and Knightrider Street, on the site of the southern end of Old Change, has been named Old Change Court to retain the memory of a part of the City's history. A new and much wider thoroughfare, called New Change, has been built on the bombed site (see New Change).

OLD JEWRY EC2 (Cheapside) E3

In 1066, When William the Conqueror seized the throne of England, he invited many of the Jewish financiers of Rouen to this country, and they settled in this area, just north of the Cheapside market. A synagogue was erected at what is now the junction of Old Jewry and Gresham Street, and a burial ground was granted to them near Aldersgate. Jewin Street and Jewin Crescent, which stood on the site of the Jews' cemetery, were destroyed in 1940 by German bombs. Up to 1100 the Jews increased in number, and the area round Old Jewry became a ghetto, with rich Jews living in the large expensive houses.

With the ascension of Henry I in 1100 their troubles began: a wave of anti-semitism swept the country, which continued through the reigns of Stephen and Henry II. In 1189 Jews were forbidden to attend the coronation of Richard I, and after the coronation thousands of them were murdered and their houses burnt. Heavy taxes were levied on them. Then came King John, who at first made friends with wealthy Jews, borrowing money from them; but when the money was not forthcoming he turned violently against them. Modern Jews have a saying 'Thank God there was only one King John'. The next monarch, Henry III, made them wear two squares of white linen as a badge upon their breasts, and built a house in Chancery Lane for Jews who wished to become Christians. Again they were subjected to heavy taxes, and those who could not pay were sent to Ireland, possibly the worst punishment of all, for Jews were hated by the Irish.

Edward I taxed them even more severely, and changed

155

their distinguishing squares from white to yellow; he also forbade them to lend money and charge interest, and finally, in the year 1291, he expelled all Jews from the country on the charge of debasing the coinage. Some 16,000 were shipped to other European countries, their ghetto in London was demolished, and the street which ran through it was named Old Jewry. When the building next door to the City of London police headquarters was destroyed in 1941 a section of 'wailing wall' was discovered.

Two churches formerly occupied the western side of the street: St Olave's stood towards the northern end (see St Olaves Court), and at the southern end, near Cheapside, stood St Mary Colechurch, which was destroyed in the Great Fire of London and was not rebuilt. Peter of Colechurch, who designed the old London Bridge, worked in this church and here Thomas à Becket was baptised. A plaque now marks the site of the church in Old Jewry.

OLD MITRE COURT EC4 (Fleet Street) A3
The court is named in memory of the Mitre Tavern, the Elizabethan hostelry where Dr Johnson, Boswell, and Oliver Goldsmith often met. The Mitre was demolished in 1829, when it was acquired by Hoare's Bank.

OUTWICH STREET EC3 (Houndsditch) G2
The street is named in memory of a thirteenth-century family called Oteswich, who built a church named St Martin Oteswich on the corner of Threadneedle Street and Bishopsgate. The church fell into disrepair towards the end of the eighteenth century, and in 1874 it was demolished to make way for the building of an office block. A plaque on the corner of Threadneedle Street marks the site of the old church.

OXFORD COURT EC4 (Cannon Street) E4
The town house of the Earls of Oxford occupied this site in the fifteenth century, and the court is named after them.

PANCRAS LANE EC4 (Queen Street) E3

The lane is named after a fourteenth-century church called St Pancras Soper Lane, which was destroyed in the Great Fire of 1666 and not rebuilt. Soper Lane was the original name of what is now Queen Street. Another church, St Benet Sherehog, stood in Pancras Lane, and this too was destroyed in the Great Fire and not rebuilt (see Sise Lane). Both churches stood on the northern side of the lane.

PANYER ALLEY EC4 (Newgate Street) D3

In medieval times the alley was inhabited by *panyers*, or makers of baskets, and a tavern called the Panyer on the Hoop stood in the alleyway which was used as a short cut to Paternoster Row.

In the nineteenth century, during excavations in Panyer Alley, a curious stone was found bearing a relief of a small boy sitting on a panyer; the words 'When ye have sought the City round yet this is still the highest ground. August 27 1688' were carved on it. Panyer Alley suffered badly in the bombing of 1941, and has now been dwarfed by the erection of the large blocks of offices and shops called Cathedral Place. The tablet of the boy on the panyer has been set in the wall of the steps connecting Panyer Alley with Cathedral Place.

PATERNOSTER ROW EC4 (St Paul's churchyard) C3

Tradition has it that this was, in medieval days, the point at which the clergy of old St Paul's began to recite the Lord's Prayer in their Corpus Christi day procession round the outside of the cathedral. The name could also have been derived from the makers of Paternoster beads who lived here.

At the extreme eastern end, near Cheapside, stood a fourteenth-century church called St Michael le Quern, a reminder of the time when this area was a cornmarket, a *quern* being a handmill or corn grinder. The church was destroyed in 1666 by the Great Fire and was not rebuilt.

In the sixteenth century Paternoster Row was famous for its many taverns, the most celebrated being the Castle, which was owned by Richard Tarleton, the comedian friend of Shakespeare. In the nineteenth century the property came into the hands of an old cook called Dolly, who made it the best-known eating place in the City, wealthy businessmen and poor clerks alike coming to Dolly's Chop House for a pint of ale and a delicious sandwich or steak—one of the attractions no doubt being the pretty waitresses Dolly employed. The premises were pulled down in 1885 for the extension of office buildings.

In the middle of the eighteenth century Paternoster Row became the centre of the book and publishing trades which had formerly operated in Little Britain, and in the nineteenth century both sides of Paternoster Row were lined with publishing houses and secondhand bookshops. The largest of the publishing houses was that of Longman, Green, Longman & Roberts, the business being founded in 1724 by Thomas Longman.

Paternoster Row was almost completely destroyed on 29 December 1940. Before the bombing it was a narrow lane, running between Ave Maria Lane and St Paul's churchyard, but now only a fragment of the eastern end remains. Paternoster Square, which occupied a part of the old Newgate market, also disappeared in the bombing, and the site is now occupied by two huge office blocks and shops; one block is called Cathedral Place and the other Paternoster Square.

PAULS PIERS WHARF EC4 (Upper Thames Street) C4

In medieval times the most sought-after property was that which lay close to the River Thames, and Upper and Lower Thames Streets were occupied by large houses, taverns, and wharves. In the fifteenth century the area south of St Benet's church passed to the Dean and Chapter of St Paul's cathedral, and a wharf was built for the unloading of all the goods bound for the cathedral. The goods were then carried up Benets Hill to Godliman Street, and thence to St Paul's.

PEMBERTON ROW EC2 (Trinity Church Passage) B3

Sir James Pemberton was Lord Mayor of London in 1611 and a prominent member of the Goldsmiths Company, which is the landlord of most of this area. A church called Holy Trinity Gough Square was erected on the northern side of Pemberton Row in 1827, but was destroyed by fire in 1842.

PEPYS STREET EC3 (Seething Lane) G4

Until 1923 the eastern end of what is now Pepys Street was called Colchester Street, but when the Port of London Authority building was erected in 1923, Colchester Street was extended to Seething Lane, and was renamed Pepys Street in honour of old Samuel Pepys: the newly built street was constructed on the exact site of the Navy Office in which Pepys was living when he recorded the events during the Great Fire of 1666. The Navy Office, situated on the eastern side of Seething Lane, was demolished in 1788.

Samuel Pepys was born in Salisbury Court, Fleet Street, in 1632, the son of a tailor, and was baptised in nearby St Bride's church. He served his apprenticeship with the Clothworkers Company and eventually reached the position of Master of that Company, which, to this day, cherishes the Loving Cup he presented to it in 1677. He became a civil servant and a MP, and eventually became Secretary of the Navy; and, as previously mentioned, was resident in the Navy Office in Seething Lane when the Great Fire of London started on 2 September 1666. His diary, in which he recorded the events during the four days of the fire, can be seen in the Public Records Office in Chancery Lane. Samuel Pepys died in 1703 in the village of Clapham, and was buried in the church of St Olave, Hart Street.

PETERBOROUGH COURT EC4 (Fleet Street) B3

In the fourteenth century this site was occupied by the house of the Bishop of Peterborough. Now the offices of the *Daily Telegraph* stand in its place.

PETERS HILL EC4 (Queen Victoria Street) D4

A fourteenth-century church called St Peter Pauls Wharf stood at the corner of Peters Hill and Upper Thames Street. The church was destroyed in the fire of 1666, and was not rebuilt.

PHILPOT LANE EC3 (Eastcheap) F4

In the fourteenth century the lane was named after Sir John Philpot, wealthy member of the Grocers Company, who became Lord Mayor in 1378. In the seventeenth century the first buildings of the East India Company stood in Philpot Lane.

PILGRIM STREET EC4 (Ludgate Hill) C3

Tradition has it that pilgrims, on their way to St Paul's cathedral, used this route from the landing stage on the old River Fleet, near the Fleet Bridge. The northern side of Pilgrim Street follows the course of the old City wall, and samples of the wall have been uncovered many times during building work on that side.

PINDAR STREET EC2 (Bishopsgate) G1

The house of Sir Paul Pindar on this site was one of the finest Elizabethan buildings in the City. Sir Paul Pindar was ambassador to Turkey in the reign of James I, and one of the wealthiest men in London, contributing nearly £10,000 towards the repairing of St Paul's cathedral. He died on the 22 August 1650, aged eighty-four, and is buried in the church of St Botolph Bishopsgate. After his death Pindar House was converted into a tavern and was called Sir Paul Pindar's Head. The tavern stood until 1891, when the need to extend the Great Eastern Railway station led to its being demolished. The original front of Sir Paul Pindar's mansion can be seen at the Victoria & Albert Museum in South Kensington.

PLAYHOUSE YARD EC4 (Blackfriars Lane) C4

In 1596 James Burbage, the actor, was granted part of the old thirteenth-century priory of the Black Friars, which he converted into a theatre, opened in 1598. William Shakespeare joined the company of the Blackfriars Theatre, and purchased a house in nearby Ireland Yard. The theatre stood until 1655, when it was pulled down and houses and streets erected on the site. Playhouse Yard was named in its memory.

PLEYDELL STREET EC4 (Bouverie Street) B3

The street is named after the landlords of this area, the Pleydell Bouveries, Earls of Radnor.

PLOUGH COURT EC3 (Lombard Street) F4

The origin of the name of this courtway is obscure, but it is almost certainly derived from a tavern of the same name. A plaque on the corner of Lombard Street marks the site of the birthplace of Alexander Pope in 1688—1 Plough Court. The house stood until 1872. Pope was the son of a linen merchant.

PLUMTREE COURT EC4 (Shoe Lane) B2

The court is another reminder of the great orchards of Sir Christopher Hatton, which took up the whole of this area in the sixteenth century (see Hatton Garden).

POPES HEAD ALLEY EC3 (Lombard Street) F3

The alley is named after a fifteenth-century tavern, the Popes Head, which stood on this site. In 1615 the Popes Head became the property of the Merchant Taylors Company, which still owns much of the property in this area. Edward

Lloyd's coffee house, the forerunner of the great Lloyd's Marine Insurance Company, stood in the alley from 1771 until 1774 when new offices were acquired in the Royal Exchange.

POPPINS COURT EC4 (Fleet Street) B3
A hostel called the Popyngaye stood on this site, the property of the Bishops of Cirencester. To this day, above the archway leading to Poppins Court, can be seen the sign of a green popinjay.

PORTSOKEN STREET E1 (Minories) H4
The street is named after the Ward in which it is situated. The Portsoken Ward consists of land which was claimed for the City by thirteen knights during the reign of King Canute. The land, which lay to the east of the City boundary, had been left uncultivated by the people living there, and the knights were granted it on condition that each of them should win three combats, one above ground, one below ground, and the last in water, and after winning these three combats should defend themselves against all comers at Smithfield. The deeds were gloriously accomplished, and the area became known as Knighten Guilde. In 1124 the Guild of Knights granted the land to the Priory of Holy Trinity, and the Ward was renamed Soke of the Port, the Port presumably being the gate, that is Aldgate, and Soke being taken from the Old English *socn*, meaning a district under a special jurisdiction. Portsoken Ward today is essentially the Jewish quarter of London, the Jews having settled here when they were allowed to return to Britain by Oliver Cromwell.

POST OFFICE COURT EC3 (Lombard Street) F4
On this site stood the mansion of Sir Robert Vyner, the wealthy goldsmith who became Lord Mayor of London in 1674. Sir Robert was a great friend of Charles II, who frequently visited him at Vyner House. A statue of Charles II,

which was presented to the City by Sir Robert Vyner, stood on the site of the old Stocks Market until 1735, when it was removed to make way for the building of the Mansion House. Sir Robert Vyner died in 1688, and shortly after his death his mansion was used to house the City's first Post Office, hence the name Post Office Court.

POULTRY EC2 (Cheapside) E3
In medieval times the people of the City bought poultry at this end of the great West Cheap market (now Cheapside).

A plaque marks the site of the birthplace of London's own poet, Thomas Hood, who was born above his father's book-shop in 1799.

St Mildred Court marks the site of a church called St Mildred's Poultry which was destroyed in the Great Fire of 1666 and rebuilt by Sir Christopher Wren, but was pulled down in 1872 to make way for bank buildings.

PRIESTS COURT EC2 (Foster Lane) D3
The courtway forms a rear entrance to the church of St Vedast for the use of its clergy, hence the name Priests Court.

PRIMROSE STREET EC2 (Bishopsgate) G1
The street is a reminder of the days when this part of the City lay almost in the suburbs, and the gardens of the house of Sir Paul Pindar stretched to the City boundary. The house and gardens were demolished when the Great Eastern Rail-way was extended (see Pindar Street).

PRINCES STREET EC2 (The Bank) E3
The street was one of the new thoroughfares constructed after the Great Fire of London, but whereas the newly built King Street and Queen Street were named after the reigning monarch, Charles II and his Queen, Catherine of Braganza, there is no apparent reason for the name of Princes Street, as the marriage produced no children.

The western side of Princes Street is taken up by bank buildings, and the main entrance to the Grocers Hall (see Grocers Hall Court). The eastern side is occupied by the huge western wall of the Bank of England.

PRINTER STREET EC4 (East Harding Street) B3
The street, and most of the surrounding area, is taken up by printing offices, which give the street its name.

PRINTING HOUSE SQUARE EC4 (Queen Victoria Street) C4
After the Great Fire of London the King's Printing House was erected on the site formerly occupied by the Blackfriars Theatre (see Playhouse Yard) and here the King's printer, John Bill, printed the Acts of Parliament, proclamations, and the speeches of Charles II. The Printing House operated until 1770. when it was removed to a site near Fleet Street.

In 1784 John Walter purchased a house in Printing House Square, and in that house, in 1785, printed a paper called the *Daily Universal Register*; on 1 January 1788 the name of the paper was changed to *The Times*. John Walter died in 1812 and was replaced by his son, John Walter the second, who caused a sensation by introducing steam-powered printing machines that could produce over 1,000 sheets an hour. *The Times* has grown to be one of the world greatest newspapers. *The Times* building suffered badly in the bombing of London, and has now been replaced by an even bigger building of which the old Printing House Square forms a forecourt.

PUDDING LANE EC3 (Eastcheap) F4
In a house on the site now occupied by 25 Pudding Lane began the Great Fire of London on Sunday, 2 September 1666; for an account of the fire see Monument Street. Although the fire started in the house of the King's baker, his trade had not given the street its name. John Stow in his sixteenth-century *Survey of London* says:

Then have ye one other lane called Rother Lane or Red Rose Lane, of such a sign there, now commonly called Pudding Lane because the butchers of Eastcheap have their scalding house for hogs there and their puddings, with other filth of beasts, are voided down that way to their dung boats on the Thames.

Times have changed: the butchers are now at Smithfield and Leadenhall markets.

PUDDLE DOCK EC4 (Upper Thames Street) C4

In medieval times horses were watered at this spot, the great puddles earning it the name Puddle Dock. The Mermaid Theatre now stands on the site, having been erected there in 1959, the only new theatre to be built in London in the last thirty years.

QUEENHITHE EC4 (Upper Thames Street) D4

From as far back as Saxon times this inlet formed a natural port or dock, and was the property of one, Eldred, and was called Eldreds Hythe. The Norman invaders recognised the importance of the dock and enlarged it. In the middle of the twelfth century the *hythe*, or haven, was given to the Queen of Henry II, so that she, by taxing the goods unloaded there, increased her personal income. Succeeding queens also made their pin money from the dock, which had, by now, been renamed the Queens Hythe. In those days the dock was the main unloading point for corn, wool, and fish, and was as important to the City as the Royal group of docks are today.

By the beginning of the sixteenth century the ships were being built much larger and found increasing difficulty in passing under London Bridge, so they began to unload their cargoes near Billingsgate, and the old dock of Queenhithe became obsolete. Today the dock is hemmed in by warehouses, but the natural square shape of the old dock can still be defined.

QUEEN STREET EC4 (Cheapside) E3

Named after Catherine of Braganza, the queen of Charles II, the thoroughfare was constructed after the Fire of 1666 to form a direct approach road to the Guildhall. An ancient City street called Soper Lane, named after the soapmakers who lived there in the thirteenth century, was widened and extended to form this new route.

QUEEN STREET PLACE EC4 (Southwark Bridge) E4

In conjunction with the aforementioned scheme of the City Corporation to form a new approach road to the Guildhall, the southern end of the approach road was connected to a thoroughfare called Broad Street, which was renamed Queen Street Place.

Immediately adjacent to Broad Street, where it joined the river, stood the Three Cranes tavern, an inn often visited by Samuel Pepys. The inn took its name from the three cranes used by the Vintners Company to lift barrels of Bordeaux wine from the ships to the warehouses. The Vintners Hall stands just to the west of Queen Street Place.

Before the bombing of the area in 1941 there stood just to the east of Queen Street Place, Three Cranes Wharf and Three Cranes Lane, but both were demolished in that bombing, and have been replaced by a multi-storey carpark and a new thoroughfare called Bell Wharf Lane.

QUEEN VICTORIA STREET EC4 (Blackfriars Bridge to the Mansion House) C4

Sir Christopher Wren first conceived the idea of a road running in line with the Thames in his plans to rebuild the City after the Fire of 1666, but it was not until 200 years later that the first steps were taken to carry out the idea. In 1867 demolition began to make way for the new street, which was to be named after Queen Victoria; property was purchased, costing £2,000,000, streets were cut in half, the Doctors Commons was demolished, as was a portion of the Heralds

166

College, and the eastern end of Knightrider Street, which was the site of the City's first fish market and was then called Old Fish Street, disappeared as the new thoroughfare swept towards Mansion House. On 4 November 1871 Queen Victoria Street was officially opened, the actual building cost being £52,000, and in 1891 the street was fitted with the first permanent electric-lighting system in the City.

Queen Victoria Street was badly damaged in the bombing of 1940–41, especially on the southern side, and much of the street had to be rebuilt. At the western end the great new building of *The Times* has been erected on the old Printing House Square. A little farther east, on the same side, is the church of St Andrew by the Wardrobe, rebuilt by Wren after the Great Fire, gutted in 1940, and restored by Marshall Sisson. Next to the church stands the British & Foreign Bible Society building, which dates from 1867. Next to Bible House are the buildings of the Post Office Telephones, which were built in 1904 and called Faraday Buildings, and from here it is possible to make a telephone call to any part of the world. On the opposite side of the road, one of the few buildings to survive the bombing is that of the London Auction Mart, the headquarters of London auctioneers.

On the corner of Godliman Street is the remaining half of the Heralds College, or College of Arms. The college stands on the site of the house of the Earls of Derby which was granted to it by Queen Mary I in 1555; the house was destroyed in the Great Fire and rebuilt by Wren in 1669. The college was incorporated by Richard III in 1484 as the official authority on all matters concerning pedigrees and coats of arms, and is divided into three sections: Garter King of Arms, who is responsible for examining all cases of arms borne illegally and the granting of new arms; Clarenceux King of Arms, who cares for all arms and pedigree descent south of the Humber; and Norroy King of Arms, who has jurisdiction of all pedigree descent north of the Humber. Opposite the College of Arms stand the newly built offices of the Salvation Army; its headquarters were formerly in Ludgate Hill but were destroyed in the bombing.

A little farther east, on the northern side, stands the church of St Nicholas Cole Abbey, the first church to be rebuilt by Sir Christopher Wren after the Fire of 1666. The church is a good example of the alterations made by the construction of Queen Victoria Street, for it originally stood in Knightrider Street, where it was hemmed in by buildings; with the construction of Queen Victoria Street the buildings on the southern side of the church were removed, thus making it appear that the church stands in Queen Victoria Street. The church was completely gutted in the bombing, but has now been restored—though the end of Knightrider Street in which it originally stood has disappeared for ever.

Next to the church is the newly erected building of the *Financial Times*, built on the site of the eastern end of Knightrider Street.

Farther east, on the same side, the bombed site on the corner of Bread Street was formerly the church of St Mildred's, destroyed in 1940. The adjacent City Fire Station was one of the few buildings to survive that bombing.

After it has crossed Cannon Street, the northern side is taken up by the church of St Mary Aldermary (see Watling Street). Opposite the church stands the huge new office block called Temple Court, in the forecourt of which can be seen the relic of the Temple of Mithras which was discovered during excavations on the bombed sites in Walbrook in 1954.

RACQUET COURT EC4 (Fleet Street) B3
Tennis (not today's lawn tennis) became very popular in the City in the reign of Charles II, and a tennis court was laid at this site; the Court is named in its memory.

RAILWAY PLACE EC3 (Fenchurch Street) G4
This is the name given to the official entrance to Fenchurch

Street railway station, erected 1882 and the first station in the City of London.

RANGOON STREET EC3 (Northumberland Alley) H4
Rangoon Street and nearby India Street are named after the East India Company, whose warehouses occupied this area. East India House stood in Leadenhall Street until 1862.

RED BULL WHARF EC4 (Upper Thames Street) E4
Named after a tavern called the Red Bull which stood here in the sixteenth century.

RED LION COURT EC4 (Fleet Street) B3
The court takes its name from the Red Lion tavern which stood here in the fifteenth century. In this court, in 1820, the *Gentleman's Magazine* was published, and it is now taken up by small printing concerns.

ROLLS BUILDINGS EC4 A3
When the Jews were deported from this country in 1291, a house erected in Chancery Lane for Jews who wished to be converted to the Christian faith fell into disuse. In 1377 Edward III had the house demolished and in its place erected a building to house the records of the reigning monarch, and also of the Inns of Chancery (see Chancery Lane). A chapel was erected in the grounds in 1617 by Inigo Jones and called St Thomas in the Rolls. Towards the middle of the nineteenth century the old Rolls Office became inadequate and was demolished, and in 1866 the new Records Office was erected on the site.

In the Rolls buildings, until recent years, were located the offices of the *Daily Mirror*, but it now has a much larger building in New Fetter Lane.

ROMAN BATH STREET EC1 (Newgate Street) D3
In the sixteenth century the name of this street was Pentecost

Lane, and here stood the numerous slaughterhouses of the butchers of the Shambles (Newgate Street).

In 1679 a Turkish merchant built the first Turkish bath in London in the street, and its name was changed to Bagnio Court, a *bagnio* being a hot bath. The name was changed again to Bath Street, and then in 1885 the Corporation added the prefix Roman, because, by then, there were many Bath Streets in the City; but why 'Roman' was considered appropriate is a mystery, for there is no record of a Roman bath ever having stood here. Today Roman Bath Street can easily be bypassed because it has been enclosed by the buildings of the General Post Office.

ROOD LANE EC3 (Eastcheap) F4

The lane derives its name from the rood, or crucifix, which stood in the churchyard of St Margaret Pattens at the corner of Eastcheap. The church was first built in the twelfth century by a family named Patin, but was destroyed in 1666 by the Great Fire. It was rebuilt in 1688 by Sir Christopher Wren but was damaged by German bombs in the spring of 1941. The church has been restored since the war, the modern parquet flooring looking somewhat out of place in the seventeenth-century surroundings. Unique to the church are the canopied pews on the western side.

ROPEMAKER STREET EC2 (Moorgate) E1

The street is named after the corders or makers of rope who lived here in the seventeenth century, and it was one of the few streets to survive the bombing of 1940 well enough to be rebuilt. Large modern office blocks have been erected on both sides of the street. Daniel Defoe, author of *Robinson Crusoe*, died in this street in 1731.

ROYAL EXCHANGE F3

The first Royal Exchange to stand on this site was founded by Sir Thomas Gresham, a City merchant who had spent several years in Belgium and long admired the Great Bourse in Antwerp. In 1563 he offered to build a comparable Exchange where City merchants could meet to conduct their business. The City Corporation accepted his offer and cleared a site for him between Cornhill and Threadneedle Street. On 7 June 1566 Sir Thomas Gresham laid the foundation stone of the City's first Exchange, and four years later, on 23 January 1571, Queen Elizabeth officially opened the building, proclaiming it the Royal Exchange. It was a long building with its main entrance fronting Cornhill, and the belltower, used for summoning merchants, was adorned by a huge grasshopper, the sign of the Greshams. In 1666 the Royal Exchange was destroyed by the flames of the Great Fire, only a statue of Sir Thomas Gresham and the Gresham grasshopper being saved.

A second Royal Exchange was designed by the City's surveyor, Edward Jerman, and the building was opened for business in September 1669. The second building was even larger than the first, and now the Gresham grasshopper surmounted the clock tower; but the second Exchange suffered the same fate as the first, being completely destroyed by fire on 10 January 1838.

The third and present Royal Exchange was opened by Queen Victoria on 28 October 1844. The architect was Sir William Tite. Statues of Sir Hugh Middleton and Sir Richard Whittington stand in niches on the northern, or Threadneedle Street, side of the Exchange, on the eastern side is a statue of Sir Thomas Gresham, and on the clock tower stands the original grasshopper of the Greshams, saved from the earlier fires. In front of the Exchange is an equestrian statue of the Duke of Wellington without stirrups, by Chantrey.

Behind the Royal Exchange is Royal Exchange Buildings, a pedestrian way built on the site of the church of St Benet Fink, which was demolished to make way for the third Royal Exchange (see Finch Lane). A statue of George Peabody the

American banker, who gave £150,000 to the poor of London, for which he received the freedom of the City, in 1862, now stands on the site of the old church.

ROYAL MINT STREET E1 (Minories) H4
The name of this street was formerly Rosemary Lane, which was changed to Rag Fair in the eighteenth century when it became famous for its fripperers or secondhand-clothes dealers. The City's poor flocked to the street to buy old clothes for themselves and their children. The Royal Mint, a sombre-looking Georgian building standing on the corner of Mansell Street, was built in 1811, outside the City boundary. Here are minted the coins of Britain and many other countries. Permission to see the coins being struck can be obtained by application to the Deputy Master of the Royal Mint.

RUSSIA COURT EC2 (Milk Street) D3
The Russia Company was formed in the sixteenth century, in the reign of Queen Mary I, to trade with Russia, and the company's offices stood on this site. The first Russian ambassador to England was sent to this country during that time and resided in Fenchurch Street.

ST ALBANS COURT EC2 (Wood Street) D2
The court is named after the church of St Alban which stood on the eastern side of Wood Street. The church is one of the oldest foundations in the City, dating back to the tenth century (see Wood Street), but only its tower remains after the bombing of 1940.

ST ALPHAGE GARDENS EC2 (Wood Street) E2
St Alphage Gardens is all that is left of the old thoroughfare called London Wall, which was completely destroyed in 1940. The City Corporation has built a new dual carriageway a little to the south of the old thoroughfare and has named that London Wall.

St Alphage Gardens was named after the church of St Alphage, whose ruin the Corporation has preserved in the new thoroughfare of London Wall. The church was built in 1777 to replace a much older church called St Mary the Virgin, which stood in the grounds of Elsynge Spital, a hospital for the blind, founded in 1331 (see London Wall). In St Alphage Gardens can be seen an excellent sample of the old Roman wall, which formerly stood in the churchyard of St Alphage.

ST ANDREWS HILL EC4 (Queen Victoria Street) C3-C4

The hill was formerly called Puddledock Hill because it led to Puddle Dock, near the present Mermaid Theatre (see Puddle Dock). When the construction of Queen Victoria Street was completed in 1871 the hill was renamed after the church of St Andrew by the Wardrobe, which stood on the side of a hill, on the northern side of Queen Victoria Street. The church was destroyed in the Great Fire of 1666; it stood originally in the vicinity of Baynards Castle, which occupied the river front in front of the church (see Castle Baynard Wharf). Wren rebuilt the church between 1685 and 1695, but it was gutted by German bombs in 1940, though it has now been completedly restored by Marshall Sisson. The suffix Wardrobe is derived from the King's Wardrobe which occupied the site next to the church (see Wardrobe Terrace).

ST ANDREWS STREET EC4 (Holborn Circus) B2

The street was constructed in the 1860s in conjunction with the building of the Holborn Viaduct, which was opened in 1869. The new thoroughfare was named after the church of St Andrew Holborn, the parish church which stands between St Andrews Street and Holborn Viaduct. The church was built in the thirteenth century, but, being in a state of decay, was rebuilt by Wren in 1686; it was, however, destroyed by German bombs in 1941 (see Holborn Viaduct).

ST BENETS PLACE EC3 (Gracechurch Street) F4

The church of St Benet Grasschurch stood at the corner of Fenchurch Street and Gracechurch Street, and the courtway is named after the church (see Gracechurch Street).

ST BOTOLPHS STREET E1 (Houndsditch) H3

The street is named after the church of St Botolph, Aldgate, standing at the corner of Houndsditch and Aldgate High Street. The original church was built in the eleventh century by the Knighten Guild, the thirteen knights who claimed this land for the City (see Portsoken Street). It escaped the Great Fire but had become so dilapidated that it was completely rebuilt by George Dance in 1741–4. Inside the church is kept a mummified head, said to be that of a Duke of Suffolk, which the clergy of the church are loath to exhibit.

ST BRIDES AVENUE EC4 (Fleet Street) B3

The avenue was built in 1825 to form a main entrance to the church of St Bride's, Fleet Street. The original church, which dated back to the thirteenth century, was destroyed by the fire of 1666, and the present church was constructed between 1670 and 1684 from a design by Wren. It has one of the most famous spires in London, originally standing 234 ft above ground; but it has been struck twice by lightning and now measures only 226 ft. In the church is buried Wynkyn de Worde, who died in 1535 and is thought to have introduced printing to Fleet Street—indeed St Bride's is often referred to as the printers' church. Also buried in the church are the poets Lovelace and Sackville, and Samuel Pepys was baptised there in 1633. Bells were added to the church in 1710.

In the 1930s, during excavations, the floor of the church collapsed, revealing a Roman burial ground dating back to the first century AD; 2,000 skeletons were taken to Cambridge University to be used for research into the origins of the British race.

The church was badly bombed in 1940, but has been superbly restored by Godfrey Allen; and two of the main features of the present church are the memorial to the Pilgrim Fathers who sailed to America in the *Mayflower* in 1620, and the altar commemorating one of their leaders who worshipped regularly in the church, Edward Winslow, later Governor of New Plymouth. In the crypt is a museum of Roman, Saxon, and other discoveries during the excavations of the 1930s.

The well of St Bridget, from which the neighbouring Bridwell Place took its name, lies beneath the present church's foundations.

ST BRIDES PASSAGE EC4 (Salisbury Square) B3

In St Brides Passage, on the left-hand side, is the Press Club of the Fleet Street journalists.

ST BRIDE STREET EC4 (Shoe Lane) B3

St Bride Street was constructed in the 1860s in conjunction with the erection of Holborn Viaduct. Before that, and before the covering-over of the River Fleet (now Farringdon Street), the main route between Fleet Street and Holborn was Shoe Lane.

ST CLEMENT COURT EC4 (Clements Lane) F4

The courtway forms an entrance to the church of St Clement, Eastcheap, one of the fifty-one churches rebuilt by Sir Christopher Wren after the Fire of 1666. The church today is almost completely hidden by Victorian office buildings.

ST DUNSTANS COURT EC4 (Fleet Street) B3

This is one of the many tiny alleyways on the northern side of Fleet Street, and is named after the church of St Dunstan-in-the-West, which stands a little farther to the west, on the same side of the street (see Fleet Street).

ST DUNSTANS HILL EC3 (Great Tower Street) G5

The hill leads to the church of St Dunstan-in-the-East, which lies in ruin on the western side of the hill, having been destroyed by German bombs in May 1941 (see Idol Lane). At night the church is a favourite haunt of City tramps.

ST GEORGES LANE EC3 (Pudding Lane) F4

At the junction of St Georges Lane and Botolph Lane stood the church of St George, which dated from the fourteenth century and was destroyed by the Great Fire. It was rebuilt by Sir Christopher Wren, only to be pulled down by the Victorian City Corporation, which often displayed little respect for historic buildings.

ST HELENS PLACE EC3 (Bishopsgate) G3

St Helens Place occupies part of the site of the priory of St Helen, which occupied the whole of this area (see Great St Helens). When Henry VIII dissolved the monasteries, St Helen's priory passed to the Leathersellers Company, which built its Hall on the site of the priory crypt. The Hall was rebuilt in 1815 and again in 1878, only to be damaged by bombs in the Second World War, and again rebuilt—number 15, St Helens Place. The company is responsible for the National Leathersellers College in Tower Bridge Road, and Colfe's Grammar School at Lewisham.

The entrance to St Helens Place is spanned by the huge buildings of the Hudson's Bay Company, which has strong connections with the Leathersellers Company.

ST JAMES PASSAGE EC3 (Dukes Place) G3

The passage name perpetuates the church of St James that stood at the corner of Mitre Square. The church, built in 1623 and dedicated to the reigning monarch, James I, was demolished in 1874, and a plaque in Mitre Square marks its site.

ST JOHNS STREET EC1 (Charterhouse Street) C1

St Johns Street, lying just outside the northern perimeter of the City boundary, recalls the name of the Priory of the Order of St John of Jerusalem which occupied this area. The Order was founded in the reign of Henry I by a baron named Jordan Briset to care for the knights wounded in the bloody battles in the Holy Land, during the years of the Crusades, and the knights were afterwards called the Knights Hospitallers. In St Johns Lane, just beyond Briset Street, can be seen, spanning the road, St Johns Gate, a relic of the old priory. The gate was re-erected in 1504 by Sir Thomas Docwra, who was Grand Prior of the Order of St John, to replace the original gate, destroyed by Wat Tyler in 1381, during the Peasants' Revolt. The priory was dissolved by Henry VIII and the property passed to the Crown, but in 1873 the old gate and the old priory church of St John's, situated in St Johns Square, passed back to the Order of St John of Jerusalem, which now uses the gatehouse as its head-quarters: the order of St John is now remembered in the St John's Ambulance Brigade.

ST KATHERINES ROW EC3 (Fenchurch Street) G4

On the eastern side of St Katherines Row can still be seen the old churchyard and railings of St Catherine Coleman, a fourteenth-century church which escaped the Fire of 1666 but became dilapidated by the middle of the eighteenth century and lay in ruins until it was demolished in 1927 to make way for Haddon House, which now occupies the site.

ST MARGARETS CLOSE EC2 (Lothbury) E3

Named after the church of St Margaret Lothbury, which stands almost opposite the northern entrance to the Bank of England. Sir Christopher Wren built this church between 1686 and 1700 to replace a fourteenth-century church destroyed in the Great Fire; inside it can be seen articles from some of the other City churches that were pulled down in the eighteenth and nineteenth centuries: the screen came from the church of All Hallows the Great, demolished in 1894 (its tower can still be seen in Cousins Lane), there are paintings of Moses and Aaron which were rescued from the church of St Christopher le Stocks (demolished in 1781 to make way for the new Bank of England building), and there is also an altarpiece from the church of St Olave, which stood in Old Jewry until being demolished in 1888.

ST MARTINS LE GRAND EC1 (Newgate Street) D3

On the eastern side, on the site now occupied by Armour House and Union House, stood the collegiate church of St Martin le Grand, first built by the Saxons in AD 750. The church was rebuilt in 1056, and two years after the crowning of William the Conqueror it and its precincts were granted the privilege of sanctuary; the grounds became a refuge for escaped prisoners and criminals sought by the law. The church was responsible for sounding the curfew bell in the evenings—announcing the closing of the City's gates, and warning people to stay indoors. St Martin le Grand was dissolved by Henry VIII and was demolished in 1548, and a number of small houses were erected in its place.

In 1818 the houses were demolished to make way for the GPO buildings, and during excavations many relics of the old church were found. The Post Office buildings were pulled down in 1913 and the office blocks called Armour House and Union House were built on the site. The General Post Office was rebuilt on the western side of St Martins le Grand, the first section being opened in 1873 and the rest of the work completed during the next twenty years. The buildings were badly damaged in 1940, but all were restored immediately after the war, except for the section at the corner of Newgate Street, which to this day lies in ruin.

Plaques on the walls of buildings facing St Martins le Grand mark the site of property demolished during the work on the present General Post Office; Bull and Mouth Street

178

was demolished in 1888, as was a French Protestant church. In Bull and Mouth Street stood a sixteenth-century inn of the same name, a corruption of Boulogne Mouth, which commemorated Henry VIII's siege of the mouth of Boulogne harbour in 1544.

ST MARY-AT-HILL EC3 (Eastcheap) F4

Formerly St Mary Hill Lane, this street was named after the church of St Mary on the Hill, which stood on its western side. The church was rebuilt by Wren between 1670 and 1676 to replace a church destroyed in the Great Fire of 1666. The interior was considerably altered in 1843 by James Savage, but the work blends excellently with that of Wren's to make it one of the City's best churches. In the 1890s Wilson Carlile, the founder of the Church Army, was rector of the church.

At number 18 is the Hall of the Watermens Company. In the days before the introduction of the hackney carriage some 40,000 boatmen plied for hire on the River Thames between Windsor and Gravesend, and the Watermens Company had jurisdiction not only over these water taxi-men but over all other persons who derived their living from the river. The Hall of the Watermens Company was formerly situated on the river, near the north end of Cannon Street railway bridge, but that Hall and all its records were lost in the Fire of 1666. The Hall was rebuilt, but in 1778 the Company moved to its present site. Today the Watermens Company works in conjunction with the Port of London Authority for the issuing of licences. Only people who have completed twelve months' apprenticeship with the company can compete in the race for Dogget's Coat and Badge, which is organised by the Fishmongers Company (see Fishmongers Hall Street).

ST MARY AXE EC3 (Leadenhall Street) G3

The name of the street is derived from a church which stood

179

on the western side, dedicated to St Mary the Virgin, and St Ursula and the Eleven Thousand Virgins. Legend has it that an ancient king of England allowed his daughter, Ursula, and her 11,000 virgin friends to take a trip to Germany, where they encountered the Huns, who, because of their dislike for virgins, took three sharp axes and cut off their heads. One of these axes was said to have been exhibited in the church of St Mary, and the lane leading to the church was called the Lane to St Mary Axe.

The church was demolished in the early sixteenth century and the parish was united to the church of St Andrew Undershaft, standing at the corner of Leadenhall Street. St Andrew Undershaft was built in the twelfth century, rebuilt between 1520 and 1532, and escaped the Great Fire of London. It derived its name from the maypole which was set up near the southern door of the church each May Day; as the maypole dwarfed the church and steeple, the church of St Andrew was said to be under the shaft. The May Day celebrations ended in 1517 on the orders of Henry VIII. The maypole, or shaft, was hung on hooks in the wall of a house in Leadenhall Street, and there it stayed until 1550, when it was dismantled and broken up. Shaft Court, in Leadenhall Street, stands on the site of the house on which the maypole was hung.

Inside the church of St Andrew Undershaft is the tomb of John Stow, whose *Survey of London*, first published in 1598, is used as a guide by all students of London's history; on his tomb he is represented as writing it. John Stow was born in 1525, the son of a tallow chandler. He did not follow his father's profession, but set himself up as a tailor near Aldgate Well (Aldgate Pump), and became a member of the Merchant Taylors Company, from whom, in later life, he received a pension, said to be £4 per year. John Stow died on 6 April 1605. At an annual Stow commemoration service inside the church, the Lord Mayor removes the quill pen from his carved hand, and a new one is put in its place. The old pen and a copy of the *Survey of London* is presented to the school which produces the best essay on London.

At 24 St Mary Axe is the Baltic Exchange, the head-quarters of all major exports and imports by sea. The Exchange, like the great Lloyd's, started its life in a coffee house, graduated to St Mary Axe in 1903, and is today recognised as one of the world's greatest produce and shipping exchanges.

ST MICHAELS ALLEY EC3 (Cornhill) F3

On the eastern side of the alley stands the church of St Michael upon Cornhill, which was rebuilt by Wren in 1670–77 to replace a twelfth-century church destroyed in the Fire of 1666. The tower was rebuilt in 1724 by Wren's pupil, Nicholas Hawksmoor.

In the narrow St Michaels Alley, on the site now occupied by the Jamaica Wine House, stood the Pasqua Rosee Coffee House, which in 1652 was the first establishment to sell coffee as a beverage in London.

ST MILDREDS COURT EC2 (Mansion House Street) E3

A church called St Mildred Poultry stood on this site. Founded by Mildred, the daughter of Merowald, a Saxon prince, the church was originally built on the banks of the River Walbrook, which was covered over in the fifteenth century. It was destroyed in the Fire, and rebuilt by Wren in 1676, but it was one of the many churches pulled down in the late nineteenth century by the City Corporation—on this occasion in 1872, to make way for the headquarters buildings of the Midland Bank.

A plaque on the corner of St Mildreds Court marks the site of the residence of Mrs Elizabeth Fry, the great nine-teenth-century prison reformer and social worker.

ST OLAVES COURT EC2 (Old Jewry) E3

A fourteenth-century church called St Olave Upwell stood

on the northern side of the court, the suffix Upwell indicating that a well lay beneath the church. The church was destroyed in the Great Fire and rebuilt by Wren in 1676, and like the previously mentioned church of St Mildred's—and so many others—was demolished in 1889 by the then Corporation. On this occasion, however, the tower and part of the churchyard was left standing, and these can be seen to this day at the Ironmonger Lane end of St Olaves Court. The ship on the steeple of the tower is a relic of the church of St Mildred Poultry.

ST PAUL'S CATHEDRAL EC4 (Ludgate Hill) C3

The first recorded cathedral to stand on this site was built in AD 603-7 by Ethelbert, King of Kent, and it was destroyed by fire in 1087. In its place was built what is now generally referred to as Old St Paul's, the building commenced in 1087 and finally finished 200 years later in 1287. Old St Paul's was much larger than the present cathedral, measuring 600 ft in length. Near the western entrance was the tiny church of St Gregory, and at the other end of the cathedral, near Paternoster Row, stood St Paul's Cross, a wooden pulpit where, for centuries, special meetings were held and important events announced. The cross was destroyed by order of Parliament in 1642. In the crypt of Old St Paul's stood another church, St Faith's. The huge spire of the cathedral, 520 ft high, was destroyed by fire in 1561, and was not rebuilt. In September 1666 the huge cathedral was destroyed in the Great Fire of London, giving the City's architect, Sir Christopher Wren, the opportunity to build it anew.

On 21 June 1675 the first stone of the new cathedral was laid, and thirty-five years later, in 1710, the work was completed. During the early excavation Wren found, at a considerable depth, sand and water mixed with seashells, and he also came across Saxon and Roman cemeteries. From early times historians had argued about the existence of a

Roman Temple of Diana lying beneath St Paul's, but Wren could find no trace of it. This did not discourage the Victorian antiquaries, who continued to mention the existence of such a temple. In 1954 a temple of Mithras was discovered just 500 yd from the cathedral, when a bulldozer was clearing the rubble from a bombed site in Walbrook.

The new St Paul's was built entirely of Portland stone in the shape of a Latin cross, and at a cost of over £700,000. The main, or western, entrance, viewed from Ludgate Hill, is world-famous. On the apex is a statue of St Paul, with St Peter on his right and St James on his left, and on the northern side of the apex is the Bell Tower, in which are housed the twelve bells presented by the twelve great City livery companies in 1878. In the southern tower, or Clock Tower, is Great Paul, one of the world's largest bells, weighing almost 17 tons; it is rung daily at 1 pm. The clock face is 17 ft in diameter, the copper hands measuring 9 ft 6 in and 5 ft in length.

In front of the cathedral steps is a statue of Queen Anne, in whose reign the cathedral was finished, and who gave thanks here for the victories of the Duke of Marlborough at Blenheim, Ramillies, and Oudenarde.

Inside the cathedral are graves and memorials second only to those of Westminster Abbey. In the crypt a portion of the old church of St Faith can still be seen, and near by are the graves of St Christopher Wren, who died in 1723, and two other architects, Robert Mylne and John Rennie. Lord Nelson, buried here in 1805, and Arthur Wellesley, Duke of Wellington, buried in 1852, occupy the places of honour. Nelson's coffin was made from the mainmast of the French flagship at the Battle of Nile, *L'Orient*. The interior of the dome is adorned by the paintings of James Thornhill depicting the life of St Paul, and the choirstalls and organ case are the work of Grinling Gibbons. Outside the church, in the north-east corner of the garden, can be seen the St Paul's Cross memorial, erected in 1910 by Sir Reginald

Blomfield on the site of the previously mentioned St Paul's Cross.

In 1925 it was discovered that the cathedral was slipping slightly to one side, no doubt because its foundations were built upon soft sand and water. *The Times* opened a fund to raise money to save it, and in the following year extensive restoration work was carried out; thousands of tons of cement were injected under pressure, into the foundations, and the cathedral was saved.

During the bombing of the City in 1940–41 St Paul's was hit on several occasions, mostly by incendiary bombs, and, considering that its surrounding area was almost completely flattened and that the building must have offered a huge target from the air, it seemed incredible that it should escape complete destruction.

ST PAUL'S CHURCHYARD EC4 (Ludgate Hill) C3

At the western end of the churchyard, where the statue of Queen Anne now stands, stood the old church of St Gregory whose bells were used to summon people to St Paul's Cross. The church was destroyed, with the cathedral, in 1666 by the Great Fire.

In the seventeenth and eighteenth centuries St Paul's churchyard was given entirely to the book trade. Where the newly built Choir House now stands, there was, until 1880, St Paul's School, founded by Dean Colet in 1509. Among its students were John Milton, the poet, the first Duke of Marlborough, and Samuel Pepys. The school was removed to Hammersmith in 1880, where it stands to this day. The new Choir House, which has recently been built, incorporates the tower of the church of St Augustine, which was destroyed by German bombs in 1941; the church stood originally on the corner of Watling Street and Old Change, and was one of Wren's churches, built in 1682. The area was completely obliterated in 1940, and the thoroughfare called Old Change no longer exists.

ST PETERS ALLEY EC3 F3

The alley surrounds the churchyard of St Peter Cornhill, which is said to be standing on the oldest consecrated ground in England. King Lucius is said to have been baptised here in the second century, 400 years before the arrival of St Augustine. The old church was rebuilt on several occasions, but was finally destroyed in the Fire of 1666. The present church was completed in 1687 by Sir Christopher Wren. Its organ dates from 1681 and was used in 1840 by Mendelssohn, the actual keyboard he used being preserved in the church. There is also a tablet commemorating what was probably one of the City's saddest events:

> James b 20 June 1773, Mary b 28 August 1774, Charles b 17 February 1776, Harriot b 10 March 1777, George b 30 January 1778, John and Elizabeth, twins b 22 March 1779 all died January 18th 1782.

They were the children of James and Mary Woodmason, who perished when their house in Leadenhall Street caught fire while their parents were at St James' Palace, celebrating the birthday of Queen Charlotte.

ST STEPHENS ROW EC4 (Walbrook) E4

St Stephen Walbrook was founded in the seventh century, built upon the bank of the River Walbrook. The church was rebuilt in 1439, but was destroyed in the Fire. The present church was completed in 1677 by Wren, who designed the dome as an experiment prior to the construction of the great dome of St Paul's cathedral.

Sir John Vanbrugh, the architect of Blenheim Palace, is buried in the family vault with the curt epitaph: 'Lie heavy on him earth for he laid many a heavy load on thee.'

Adjoining the church is a small building erected by the Samaritans, a voluntary society formed to help those in despair.

ST SWITHINS LANE EC4 (Cannon Street) E4

The church of St Swithin, at the western corner of St

Swithins Lane and Cannon Street, was built in 1687 by Wren to replace the church destroyed in the Great Fire. In 1798 the London Stone, the stone from which the Romans measured distances, was inserted into the wall of the church, facing Cannon Street (see Cannon Street); it had previously occupied a site on the southern side of Cannon Street, opposite the church. In 1940 the church and most of St Swithins Lane was destroyed by German bombs, and in 1960 the ruins of the church were sold, and the Bank of China erected on its site. The London Stone has been inserted into the wall of the bank, covered by a cage in almost the same position as it was in the old church of St Swithins.

The western side of St Swithins Lane is taken up by the huge St Swithin's House, built since the war. Incorporated in the building is the new Hall of the Founders Company, built to replace the one destroyed in the bombing. The Founders were originally sited in Lothbury (see Founders Court), and moved to their present site in 1845. From the sixteenth century the Founders were given the responsibility of making the brass weights used by the City's grocers, and they stamped all approved weights with the company's mark. They were also responsible for investigations into false weights, work now carried out by the Department of Weights & Measures. Today the Founders Company is connected with the country's iron foundries, and the giving of awards for research into metallurgy.

The headquarters of the great banking house of Rothschild is located in St Swithins Lane, in New Court.

SALISBURY COURT EC4 (Fleet Street) B3

This thoroughfare formerly led to Salisbury House, the London residence of the Bishops of Salisbury. At number 13, on the eastern side, a plaque marks the site of the birthplace of Samuel Pepys, who recorded the events of the Great Fire of London; he was born in his father's tailor's shop in 1632 (see Pepys Street).

SALISBURY SQUARE EC4 (Salisbury Court) B3

The square occupies the site of the residence of the Bishops of Salisbury, built in 1380 and called Salisbury House. In 1611 the property passed to the Earl of Dorset, and the name was changed to Dorset House; it was demolished in 1613.

A plaque on the side of modern Salisbury Square House marks the site of the Salisbury Court Playhouse which was built in 1629 and destroyed in 1649.

In the early eighteenth century Salisbury Square was the scene of the Mug House Riots. When Queen Anne died in 1714 she left no direct heir, and her successor was George, the son of the elector of Hanover, who became king in 1714. But his accession was opposed by the Tory party, who supported the Jacobite cause. The Whig party, however, preferred George, and a number of free-and-easy clubs were opened where Whig supporters would meet regularly and drink ale. The mugs from which they drank were moulded to resemble the face of Lord Shaftesbury, the Whig leader (it is from these mugs that the expression 'ugly mug' is derived). The Tories made several raids on these Mug Houses, and the one on Read's Mug House in Salisbury Square in July 1716 was so violent that it ended in five men being hung at Tyburn.

SALTERS COURT EC4 (Bow Lane) D4

Before the introduction of refrigeration, salt was the only means of preserving fish and meat, and the Salters Company was, for nearly 500 years, responsible for supplying the salt used for this purpose. The company's first Hall was erected on this site in 1454, presumably to be near the fish market, which was situated at the southern end of Friday Street. The Salters Hall was destroyed by fire on a number of occasions, and in 1641 moved to new premises near St Swithin's church in Cannon Street.

SALTERS HALL COURT EC4 (Cannon Street) E4

This courtway formerly led to the Hall of the Salters Company, which moved to this site in 1641. The Hall was destroyed in the bombing of 1940 and the courtway has been named to commemorate it.

SARACENS HEAD YARD EC3 (Jewry Street) G3

The Saracens Head was a well-known City coaching inn from which coaches ran regularly to East Anglia. As late as 1750 people gathered here to watch the travellers boarding the stage coaches for Yarmouth, a journey which took twenty hours.

SAVAGE GARDENS EC3 (Trinity Square) G4

Named after Sir Thomas Savage, whose house stood on Tower Hill in the early seventeenth century.

SEACOLE LANE EC4 (Farringdon Street) C3

In medieval times, when the River Fleet flowed where Farringdon Street now runs, the barges bringing coal to the City sailed up the Fleet to this point, and here unloaded their cargoes of sea-coal.

SEETHING LANE EC3 (Byward Street) G4

The name is corrupted from the Old English word *ceafen*, meaning chaff, for chaff was blown across here when neighbouring Fenchurch Street was a cornmarket. The name of the street in the sixteenth century was Sything Lane, and it was changed to its present form in the seventeenth century.

Seething Lane has strong associations with Samuel Pepys, who lived in the old Navy Office which occupied the eastern side of the street, and it was from his bedroom in this office that he began recording the events of the Great Fire of London (see Pepys Street).

In 1777 Horatio Nelson lived at the Navy Office when he was taking his officer's examinations. The old Navy Office was demolished in 1788, and in 1923, when the present Port of London Authority building was erected, a new thoroughfare was constructed on the site of the Navy Office and was named Pepys Street.

SERJEANTS INN EC4 (Fleet Street) B3
There were originally two inns belonging to the Serjeants at Law, one in Chancery Lane, near Cliffords Inn, and the other in Fleet Street, where it is still remembered in name only. The Serjeants at Law were a special type of barrister from whose ranks the judges were chosen, and were distinguished by their peculiar head-dress, or *coif*, a close-fitting cap of white silk. The Order of the Coif, or Serjeants at Law, was abolished in the late eighteenth century. The inn in Chancery Lane was demolished in 1878 and the one in Fleet Street a little later.

SERMON LANE EC4 (Carter Lane) D4
Sermon Lane was formerly called Sheremoniers Lane from the sheremongers who sheared, or cut and rounded, the silver plates used in the minting of coins.

According to John Stow's *Survey of London* there stood in the lane, in the thirteenth century, a building called Blacke Loft, where the silver was melted down. The king's bullion store stood near by (see Old Change). The area was badly bombed in 1940, as can be seen by the new office blocks which have, in recent years, been erected on the bombed sites.

SHAFTESBURY PLACE EC1 (Aldersgate Street) D2
On this site stood the house of Anthony Ashley Cooper, first Earl of Shaftesbury. The house, one of the finest in the City, was built in 1644 by Inigo Jones for the Earl of Thanet; he later sold it to the Earl of Shaftesbury, who lived here until 1683. Shaftesbury House was converted into an inn in the eighteenth century, then later a hospital, and was demolished in 1882.

At the eastern end of Shaftesbury Place stands the Hall of the Ironmongers Company. In the fourteenth century the Ironmongers were situated near Old Jewry, where they are still remembered in Ironmonger Lane, but in 1457 the company, due to the increased demand for iron and steel rods, built a new Hall in Fenchurch Street, near Billiter Street. The Hall was rebuilt on several occasions, the last time in 1745, but this building was destroyed by a German bomb in 1917. The company moved to its present site in 1923 and the magnificent Tudor-style Hall was opened in 1925; it suffered some damage in the bombing of 1940 but is now fully restored.

SHAFTS COURT EC3 (Leadenhall Street) G3
On the site of this court stood the house upon which hung the great maypole used in the May Day celebrations (see St Mary Axe).

SHERBOURNE LANE EC4 (King William Street) E4
John Stow in his *Survey of London*, says that at this point the River Langbourne turned south to the Thames, breaking into small shares or streams. The existence of the River Langbourne is refuted by modern historians, and the name is said to be derived from Shitteborwe Lane, the shittah being a tree of the acacia family.

SHOE LANE EC4 B2
The origin of the name of this lane is uncertain, but there was in ancient times a well situated here called Showelle, and it is from this that the name is probably derived.

Before the construction of Holborn Viaduct in 1869, Shoe Lane was the main route between Fleet Street and the Holborn Valley, running parallel with the old River Fleet. With the construction of the Viaduct and St Andrews Street and Bride Street, Shoe Lane is now almost a forgotten thoroughfare. The narrow southern end is flanked by the *Daily Express* and the *Daily Telegraph* buildings, the northern end disappears under Holborn Viaduct, and even here the street is taken up by the newspaper vans of the London *Evening Standard*.

The old main entrance of St Andrew's church can be seen on the western side (see Holborn Viaduct), and at this point the steepness of the old Holborn Valley can be seen.

SILK STREET EC2 (Moor Lane) E2

The silk weaving in London in the seventeenth century was carried out by the French protestant refugees who settled in the area now known as Spitalfields Market. By the nineteenth century many English silk weavers had come down from the north of England to join the old French families, and to start up silk factories. Many of the English silk manufacturers lived in this street, and it was eventually named after them.

In 1940 the first bombs to fall on the City completely demolished the whole of this area, and today from the newly built Silk Street one can look southwards on to the wide-open spaces where bomb damage is still evident, and new skyscraper office blocks rise rapidly from nothing.

SISE LANE EC4 (Queen Victoria Street) E3

A church called St Benet Sherehog stood at the corner of Sise Lane and Pancras Lane; it was originally dedicated to St Osyth and St Benet, and the little lane leading to the church was called St Syth Lane, which has been corrupted to Sise Lane. The suffix Sherehog is a corruption of Benedict Shorne, a member of the Fishmongers Company who rebuilt the church in the fourteenth century; the church was destroyed in the Fire of 1666 and was not rebuilt.

Only the northern end of Sise Lane remains today; the southern end was destroyed in the bombing of 1941, and Temple Court has been erected on the site.

SKINNERS LANE EC4 (Queen Street) D4

Before World War II the street was known as Maiden Lane,

but its name was changed to Skinners Lane because the whole of the surrounding area is given to the fur trade. Pelts can be seen in the little shops on both sides of the lane, and furriers, conversing in many languages, can be seen on the street corners. The Skinners Hall is in Dowgate Hill, and the auction rooms of the Hudson's Bay Company are in nearby Garlick Hill.

SNOW HILL EC1 (Holborn Viaduct) E2

In the seventeenth century, long before the construction of Holborn Viaduct, east-to-west travellers arriving at New Gate would be faced with the steep descent of Snow Hill, crossing the River Fleet by Holborn Bridge, and then going up Holborn Hill.

Snow Hill is said, debatably, to be a corruption of Snore Hill—the passengers arriving at the Saracens Head after a long journey would invariably be asleep and snoring.

The Saracens Head dated from the early twelfth century when Richard the Lionheart, returning from the Crusades, rested at the tavern and gave the proprietor permission to call it by that name. The old tavern was wiped out in the Great Fire, and a much larger one was built; it became one of the City's important coaching inns, from which coaches set off on the long journeys to the north of England. A plaque on the front of Snow Hill police station marks the site of the tavern, which was demolished in 1868.

John Bunyan, author of *Pilgrim's Progress*, died in a tavern called the Star on Snow Hill in 1688. At the foot of the hill stood a conduit, a communal watering point; the conduit was rebuilt in the late sixteenth century by William Lamb, who is remembered in Lambs Conduit Street, Holborn.

SOUTH PLACE EC2 (Moorgate) F2

South Place was built in 1789 at the same time as Finsbury Square, and, as it lay in the south of the square, was named simply South Place. In the early 1900s both corners of the junction of Dominion Street and South Place were occupied by hotels: on the site of the present post office stood Armfields Hotel, and on the opposite corner, where Grobbs restaurant now stands, was the Metropolitan Hotel.

STAINING LANE EC2 D2

A church called St Mary Staining stood on the corner of Oat Lane, and was said to be dedicated to the men from Staines who came to work in the City in the fourteenth century, though for what reason seems to be forgotten. On the western side of the lane stands the Hall of the Haberdashers Company. The Haberdashers, eighth of the twelve great City livery companies, acquired this site for their first Hall in 1478, their members being very active in the West Cheap (Cheapside) market, where they controlled many of the stalls selling all types of small wares, such as pins, tapes, ribbons and combs. Their great rivals were the Mercers, who sold similar items. The orignal Hall of the Haberdashers was destroyed in the Fire of 1666 and a new Hall was built, but this too was destroyed by the bombing of 1940, being rebuilt in 1956. Today the Company administers about eighty charities and supports schools all over Britain. Staining Lane was completely destroyed in the bombing of 1940 and, like the surrounding area, has been completely rebuilt.

STAR ALLEY EC3 (Mark Lane) G4

The alley was named after an ancient tavern called the Star, in Mark Lane. On the corner of Star Alley and Mark Lane can be seen the tower of All Hallows Staining, the first church in the City to be built of *stane*, or stone (see Mark Lane). Queen Elizabeth I visited the church to give thanks for her release from the Tower in 1554; she then proceeded to the Kings Heade tavern where she dined on pork and peas.

STATIONERS HALL COURT EC4 (Ludgate Hill) C3

The small alley wedged between St Martin's church and the

newly built Colonial Mutual House leads to the Hall of the Stationers and Newspaper Makers. In 1611 the company purchased a large old house that had been occupied by nobility since the fourteenth century, and this it converted into its first Hall; for 300 years the titles of all books published by members were registered here for copyright purposes. The present Hall dates from 1670, the original having been destroyed in the Great Fire, and though it suffered considerable damage in the bombing of 1941 it has now been completely restored. The company still possesses the complete register of books, among which are the first folio of Shakespeare (1623), Milton's *Pardise Lost* (1667) and Dr Johnson's *Dictionary* (1775).

STEW LANE EC4 (Upper Thames Street) D4
From the twelfth to the seventeenth century licensed brothels, called stews or bordellos, were numerous along the banks of the Thames, and one such house stood on this site. The majority of stews, however, lay across the river on Bankside, between London and Southwark bridges. There the Bishops of Winchester, whose own residence occupied a large area near Southwark Cathedral, leased as many as twenty of their houses for the purposes of prostitution.

STOTHARD PLACE EC2 (Bishopsgate) G1
Thomas Stothard was born at the Black Horse in Long Acre in 1755, and he became a famous illustrator of books. He served a seven-year apprenticeship as a draughtsman in brocade silk in nearby Spital Square, reaching the height of his fame in the nineteenth century when he won a competition to design the Waterloo Shield, which was presented to the Duke of Wellington to commemorate his famous victory at Waterloo. He died in 1834 and is buried in Bunhill Cemetery, City Road.

SUFFOLK LANE EC4 E4
The Duke of Suffolk resided in a house situated at the end of

194

the lane which was originally built by Lord Mayor Sir John
Pountney in the fourteenth century, and was then called the
Manor of the Rose. The house, referred to by Shakespeare
in his *King Henry VIII*, was purchased by the Merchant Taylors Company in 1561, and converted into a school; it stood
here for over 300 years, and was eventually demolished in
1875 when the Company erected a new school in the grounds
of Charterhouse. This school was removed from Charterhouse in 1935 and now occupies 250 acres in Northwood,
Middlesex.

SUGAR LOAF COURT EC4 (Garlick Hill) D4
In the sixteenth century the City's ancient main dock,
Queenhithe, began handling the boats bringing sugar to the
City, and in Sugar Loaf Court stood the shops and ware-
houses where the sugar was sold and stored.

SWAN LANE EC4 (Upper Thames Street) E5
A famous City tavern called the Old Swan stood at the river
end of this lane. Boat passengers not wishing to risk the
rapids under London Bridge disembarked at Old Swan
stairs. The race for Dogget's Coat and Badge (see Fishmongers Hall Street) was originally run from the Old Swan,
London Bridge, to the Old Swan at Chelsea.

The lane was completely destroyed by the bombing of
1941, and the whole of the western side is now taken up by a
multi-storey car park. At the river end is a pleasant little
jetty where City workers can enjoy a lunchtime view of
London Bridge and the Thames.

TALBOT COURT EC3 (Gracechurch Street) F4
This court was named after a tavern called The Talbot which
stood on the site; the talbot, a huge dog used for hunting,
was a common inn sign in medieval times. The tavern was
destroyed in the Great Fire of 1666.

TALLIS STREET EC4 (John Carpenter Street) B4

Thomas Tallis, the sixteenth-century composer of church music, who died in 1585, is buried in St Alphage church, Greenwich. His name is remembered here because the Guildhall School of Music stands in the adjacent John Carpenter Street.

TANFIELD COURT EC4 (Temple) A4

Sir Lawrence Tanfield was a famous lawyer who became Chief Baron of the Exchequer in the reign of James I. He lodged in this court in 1607, and when he died in 1625 the court was named after him.

TELEGRAPH STREET EC2 (Moorgate) E3

The first telegraph office of the Central Post Office occupied this site until 1873, when it was removed to the newly built General Post Office buildings in St Martin's le Grand.

TEMPLE EC4 (between Fleet Street and Victoria Embankment) A4

The Knights Templars were formed in the twelfth century to guard pilgrims on the dangerous roads in the Holy Land. They built their first headquarters in High Holborn, near Chancery Lane, and moved to the present site near the river in 1184. The building of Chancery Lane is attributed to the Knights Templars, who constructed it in order to transport their belongings to the new site. Here they built their round church and divided the property into three sections, the Inner, Middle and Outer Temples. The Order of the Knights Templars was dissolved in 1312 and the Inner and Middle Temples passed to the Order of St John of Jerusalem, who eventually leased it to the students of law (see Inner Temple and Middle Temple). The Outer Temple was granted to the Bishop of Exeter, who built his London residence there (see Essex Court).

THAVIES INN EC4 (St Andrew Street) B2

In 1348 John Thavie, a member of the Armourers Company, leased this property to the students of law, and in the early sixteenth century it was purchased by the benchers of Lincolns Inn, who remembered the original owner and named it Thavies Inn. The inn was sold in 1771 to a private developer who erected a block of offices. The whole area was wiped out by German bombs in 1941, but John Thavie has not been forgotten, for his name has been retained in the naming of the new office blocks erected on the site.

THREADNEEDLE STREET EC2 (The Bank) F3

The Merchant Taylors Company, whose Hall stands at number 30, is responsible for the naming of this street. The arms of the company include three needles, and the street was originally Three Needles Street.

The Merchant Taylors Company acquired the present site in 1347 and built its Hall about that time. That Hall was destroyed in the Great Fire of 1666 and a new one was erected in 1671; in 1844 this was altered and enlarged, and it was destroyed by German bombs in 1940. The Hall is now fully restored and is one of the finest in the City.

In medieval times the Merchant Taylors' greatest rivals were the Skinners, and in 1484 their quarrels led to bloodshed. The dispute was taken to the Lord Mayor, Sir Robert Billesden, who decreed that to end the quarrelling the Master of one company should entertain the Master of the other at dinner, annually. To this day the custom is observed: the Skinners dine with the Taylors in July, and in August the Taylors dine with the Skinners. Lord Mayor Billesden also decreed that each company should rank as sixth or seventh in alternate years, and this too is still observed; it is from this Billesden Award, as it is called, that we derive the expression 'to be at sixes and sevens'. The Merchant Taylors school which had stood in the City since 1561 was moved in 1935 to Northwood in Middlesex.

On the same side of the street, at the corner of Bishopsgate, a plaque marks the site of the church of St Martin Outwich, which was built by a family named Oteswich, and stood here until 1874, when, in a state of collapse, it was demolished to make way for a new bank building. The family Oteswich, corrupted to Outwich, is remembered in Outwich Street in Houndsditch.

Opposite the church, on the other corner of the street, stood South Sea House, the headquarters of the South Sea Company (see Change Alley); the site is now occupied by the buildings of the Bank of Scotland. Three more churches graced Threadneedle Street: on the corner of Finch Lane, the church of St Benet Fink, rebuilt by Wren in 1673, was demolished in 1844 to make way for the enlarging of the Royal Exchange (see Finch Lane); on the corner of Bartholomew Lane a plaque marks the site of St Bartholomew by the Exchange, another Wren church, which was demolished in 1841 to accommodate the Sun Life Insurance Company's buildings; and the third church stood on the site now occupied by the Bank of England (it was called St Christopher le Stocks because it stood opposite the old Stocks Market, now the site of the Mansion House). The church was rebuilt by Wren after the Great Fire, but was demolished in 1794 to make way for the new Bank of England.

The idea of a Bank of England was conceived by a Scotsman named William Paterson in 1690, and from that time until 1734 the Bank carried out its business in the Hall of the Grocers Company, having been recognised by Parliament in 1694. In 1734 the first Bank of England building was erected on the present site, but this soon became inadequate, and in 1788 a huge new building was designed by Sir John Soane. The new bank was completed in 1833, but today all that remains of it are the fortress-like walls. The present building was constructed between the wars, and was completed in 1939, the architects being Sir Herbert Baker and F. W. Troup. A statue of Sir John Soane can be seen in the wall on the northern side of the bank, and inside the building the old churchyard of St Christopher le Stocks has been converted into a central garden.

The nickname 'the old lady of Threadneedle Street' was acquired in the early nineteenth century. In 1811 a young clerk in the bank, named Philip Whitehead, made an attempt to forge cheques, but was discovered, and for his crime was executed at Newgate Prison. His young sister, Sarah, was so shocked at the news of his execution that she mentally refused to accept it, and visited the bank daily over twenty-five years, always asking after her brother. The bank clerks each time found a suitable excuse for his absence, and as the years rolled by they referred to her as 'the old lady of Threadneedle Street'.

THREE KINGS COURT EC4 (Fleet Street) B3
Here stood The Three Kings, one of the many taverns in Fleet Street. It was destroyed in the Fire of 1666, the last flames dying out about 100 yd west of this site.

THREE NUNS COURT EC2 (Aldermanbury) E2
The courtway formerly led to the church of St Michael Bassishaw, a thirteenth-century church that was wiped out in the Great Fire and was rebuilt by Wren. The church was demolished in 1899 to make way for an office block called Bassishaw House, which in turn was destroyed in the bombing of 1940. A new building has been erected, housing the City of London Exhibition Hall.

THROGMORTON AVENUE EC2 (London Wall) F3
The avenue was constructed in 1875 and cut through the gardens of the Drapers Company, which until that time was one of the quiet retreats of the City.

On the corner of the avenue and London Wall stands the Hall of the Carpenters Company which has occupied this site since 1429. The old Hall escaped the Great Fire, but being in a state of decay was demolished when Throgmorton Avenue was under construction; a new Hall was built in 1877, but this was completely destroyed in the bombing of 1941, and in its place was built the present Hall.

After the 1939–45 war the Carpenters Company aided the Government by setting up training establishments for demobilised men who wished to take up carpentry as a profession.

THROGMORTON STREET EC2 (Old Broad Street) F3

The street is named after Sir Nicholas Throgmorton, ambassador and friend of Queen Elizabeth I. Sir Nicholas died in 1571 in the house of Robert Dudley, the Earl of Leicester, who was Queen Elizabeth's favourite, and although it was never proved it is strongly believed that Throgmorton was poisoned by Dudley. Sir Nicholas Throgmorton was buried in the church of St Catherine Cree, Leadenhall Street.

Throgmorton Street today is one of the City's best-known streets, where, during the working day the activities of the Stock Exchange are in full swing. The Stock Exchange takes up the whole of the southern side of the street (see Capel Court).

On the corner of Throgmorton Avenue stands the Hall of the Drapers Company. Their first Hall was erected in this area in 1541, on the site of the house of Thomas Cromwell, but the Hall and the remaining parts of the mansion were destroyed in the Great Fire. A new Hall was erected in 1677, and although additions were made in 1774 and again in 1870, and considerable damage was inflicted in 1940, parts of the seventeenth-century work can still be seen.

In the fifteenth and sixteenth centuries the Drapers Company was prominent in the Cheapside Market, its many stalls selling all types of dyed cloth. It ranks third in precedence among the City livery companies.

TOKENHOUSE YARD EC2 (Lothbury) E3

The yard takes its name from an early seventeenth-century

house that minted tokens for many of London's tradesmen. The tokens, or farthings, as they were called, were the forerunners of our present monetary system.

TOOKS COURT EC4 (Furnival Street) A2
Benjamin Tooks, Queen Anne's printer, lived in a house near this site in 1713.

THE TOWER EC3 (Tower Hill) H5
The Tower of London lies outside the City boundary, in the borough of Tower Hamlets, and derives its name from the White Tower, which stands in the middle of the present fortress. The White Tower was completed in 1097 by Gundulf, Bishop of Rochester, for William the Conqueror to use as a royal residence and a prison. The White Tower was further fortified in the thirteenth century when it was surrounded by a huge protecting wall containing twelve more towers. Additions were made by successive monarchs, and by the reign of Henry VIII the present fortress was completed.

The official title of the Tower is Her Majesty's Royal Fortress and Palace of the Tower of London, but it has not been used as a residence by royalty since the reign of James I. It is as a prison and execution centre that the Tower is best known, and most of the towers have, at some time, been used as prisons or torture chambers; in the Beauchamp Tower the inscriptions of some of its inmates can still be seen on the walls. The chapel of the church of St Peter ad Vincula contains the remains of many of those who were executed within the Tower itself or outside on Tower Hill; plaques mark both execution sites, one on Tower Green, inside the Tower, and the other a little to the west of the Merchant Navy Memorial on Tower Hill.

The remains of the two princes who were murdered in the Bloody Tower in 1483 were discovered in 1647 and were later transferred to Westminster Abbey by order of Charles II.

One of the main attractions of the Tower are the Crown jewels, which are kept in the Wakefield Tower. The present ticket office stands on the site of the Lion Tower, where lions and other fierce animals were kept as an added protection, until it was demolished in 1834: the animals were taken to Regent's Park, and were used to start up the Zoological Gardens.

TOWER ROYAL EC4 (Cannon Street) E4
On this site stood an old palace which was used as a royal residence by King Stephen in the twelfth century; it was later used by the wife of the Black Prince, and was known as the Queen's Wardrobe. The old palace fell into decay, and was finally destroyed in the Great Fire of London. The suffix Royal came about in the early fourteenth century from the French vintners who lived in the area and called their street La Riole, after the French town near Bordeaux whence they came. The old palace was then called La Tour Riole, but has since been corrupted to its present form (see College Hill).

TRIG LANE EC4 (Upper Thames Street) D4
In the reign of Edward III a rich City merchant named John Trigge built himself a fine mansion here. The buildings were destroyed by the Great Fire, and the site is now occupied by warehouses.

TRINITY CHURCH PASSAGE EC4 (Fetter Lane) A3
The passage was constructed in 1827 to make an entrance to a new church, Holy Trinity, designed by J. Shaw. The church occupied the site between Great New Street and Pemberton Row, and just a few years after its completion was destroyed by fire. In 1880 its remains were sold to a development company, which erected an office building on the site.

TRINITY COURT EC1 (Aldersgate Street) D2

At the western end of the courtway stood a medieval chapel called Holy Trinity which was pulled down in 1796, but the entrance-way survived, and the name Trinity Court perpetuates the old building. The Victorian houses either side of Trinity Court were among the few to survive the bombing of 1940.

TRUMP STREET EC2 (King Street) E3

In medieval times the trumpet and horn makers, who supplied instruments for civic occasions, lived here, and it was called Trumpadere Street. It was obliterated by bombing on 29 December 1940, and has since been completely rebuilt.

TUDOR STREET EC4 (New Bridge Street) B4

The street formerly led to the great palace of Bridewell which occupied the whole of the area between St Bride's church and the River Thames, and was protected on its eastern side by the River Fleet (now New Bridge Street). The palace was built as a royal residence for Henry VIII, but his son, Edward VI, converted it into an orphanage (see Bridewell Place). Both Henry VIII and Edward VI being Tudors, the street was called Tudor Street. Today Tudor Street is given over entirely to the newspaper industry, and the vans of the London *Evening News* line both sides. At the extreme western end is the eastern gateway to the Temple.

TURNAGAIN LANE EC4 (Farringdon Street) B2

In medieval times, long before the construction of Holborn Viaduct, when this lane was a pleasant walk between Snow Hill and the River Fleet, there was no bridge at this point and pedestrians were often forced to retrace their steps—so the lane became known as Turnagain Lane. It was cut in half in 1869 when Holborn Viaduct was erected.

TURNERS ALLEY EC3 (Eastcheap) F4

The Hall of the Turners Company stood on this site up until
the Great Fire of London, for during the fire it was severely
damaged and later demolished.

UPPER THAMES STREET EC4 (Blackfriars Underpass to
London Bridge) C4

Thames Street, running parallel with the River Thames from
the Tower of London to the Blackfriars monastery, was in
medieval times the longest thoroughfare in the City, and,
because of its location near the river, was inhabited by the
City's wealthy people. Towards the end of the eighteenth
century the street was divided into two sections: the portion
between the Tower and London Bridge was called Lower
Thames Street, and the section between London Bridge and
Blackfriars was named Upper Thames Street.

At the western end of Upper Thames Street, where the
Mermaid Theatre now stands, stood Puddle Dock (page
165). Immediately next to Puddle Dock was Baynards Castle,
destroyed in the Fire of 1666 (see Castle Baynard Wharf).

Opposite the eastern end of Baynard Castle stood the
church of St Benet Paul's Wharf, which was consumed by the
flames of the Great Fire, was rebuilt by Wren in 1685, and,
having survived the bombing of the last war, still stands (see
Benets Hill).

A little to the east, on the corner of Peters Hill, stood the
church of St Peter Paul's Wharf which was destroyed in the
Great Fire and not rebuilt (see Peters Hill).

A little farther to the east stood the church of St Mary
Somerset, which was also lost in the Fire of 1666. Wren
rebuilt it in 1695, but it was demolished in 1872 when
Upper Thames Street was widened; the tower, however,
was left as a reminder, and it can still be seen standing amid
the bomb damage opposite Broken Wharf.

Farther east, opposite the medieval dock of Queenhythe,
stood yet another church, St Michael Queenhythe; like the

204

other churches it was destroyed by the Fire; rebuilt by Wren, it was only to be demolished in 1875 to make way for office buildings.

East of the site of St Michael Queenhythe, with its entrance in Dowgate Hill, stands the church of St James Garlickhythe; the original was destroyed by the Great Fire, and the present church is the work of Wren who rebuilt it between 1674 and 1687. It was badly hit by German bombs in World War II, but is now fully restored.

Opposite St James Garlickhythe is the Hall of the Vintners Company, which has occupied this site since 1357 (see Vintners Place).

East of the Vintners Hall stood the wharf of the Bordeaux wine merchants, who used three great beams to hoist the wine casks from the ships to the shore. A tavern erected on the site of the old wharf, Three Cranes in the Vintry, was a popular meeting place for authors and actors in the sixteenth and seventeenth centuries. Before the bombing of this area in World War II, Three Cranes Lane ran down to the river immediately adjacent to Queen Street Place; a multi-storey car park has been erected in its place, and Three Cranes Lane has disappeared for ever.

Opposite this site stood another church, called St Martin Vintry, which was consumed by the flames of the Great Fire and was not rebuilt; St Martin is the patron saint of the Vintners Company.

The bombing of 1941 has laid bare this side of Upper Thames Street, and for the first time for centuries Wren's church of St Michael Paternoster Royal is fully exposed; the suffix 'Royal' is a corruption of La Riole, a small town near Bordeaux whence many of the workers in the wine trade originally came, and shows the extent to which the wine trade dominated this area (see College Hill).

Farther east, the buildings of Cannon Street railway station stand on the site of two more churches. All Hallows the Great was destroyed in the Great Fire and was rebuilt by Wren; it was, however, demolished in 1894 to make way for Cannon Street station, though the tower was saved, and can still be seen on the eastern side of the station. All Hallows the Less, the smaller of the two churches, was also obliterated by the Great Fire, and was not considered worth rebuilding. The station also covers part of the site of the ancient German steelyard, belonging to the Hanse Merchants who dominated the European steel market until the seventeenth century.

On the northern side of Upper Thames Street, the names Laurence Pountney Lane, Ducksfoot Lane, and Suffolk Lane all perpetuate successive owners of a large mansion and gardens which occupied the whole of this area. The mansion was built in the fourteenth century and became the home of Sir Laurence Pountney, the Lord Mayor; it was known then as Pountney's Inn. The property then passed to the Earl of Essex, and after that was used by Prince Hal, the future Henry VIII. The mansion fell into decay in the sixteenth century and was demolished and the area near the river became known as Cold Harbour. The Duke of Suffolk built his house in what used to be the gardens of Pountney's Inn, and this house is mentioned in Shakespeare's *King Henry VIII* as the Manor of the Rose. In 1561 the mansion was acquired by the Merchant Taylors Company, which converted it into a school (see Suffolk Lane).

At the extreme end of Upper Thames Street, almost under the arches of London Bridge stands the Fishmongers Hall (see Fishmongers Hall Street).

VICTORIA AVENUE EC2 (Bishopsgate) G2

The City of London police station was built in Bishopsgate in 1901, and the side entrance to the station was named after Queen Victoria, who died on 22 January 1901, having reigned for sixty-four years.

VICTORIA EMBANKMENT EC4 (Blackfriars Bridge) A4

The need for another thoroughfare to connect the City with Westminster came with the increase in road traffic during the early nineteenth century, for the east-to-west routes of Fleet Street and Holborn were becoming congested by horse-drawn vehicles, both commercial and private. In 1864 the plans of Sir Joseph Bazalgette to cut a connecting road through, directly adjacent to the River Thames, were put into operation, with the result that nearly thirty-eight acres of land were claimed from the river, and a new thoroughfare appeared on the map of London. The road was opened in 1870 and called the Victoria Embankment in honour of the reigning monarch.

The Embankment enters the City boundary at The Temple, where the two dragons of St George mark the western perimeter. These monuments formerly adorned the Coal Exchange which stood on the corner of St Mary at Hill and Lower Thames Street, and they were removed to the present site in 1963 when the Coal Exchange was demolished. On the northern side the beautiful gardens of the Temple extend to Temple Avenue, and on the railings of the gardens, near the dragon of St George, is a plaque commemorating the last visit to the City of Queen Victoria in March 1900. Opposite the Temple Gardens is a memorial to the men of the British Navy who lost their lives in submarines during the two World Wars. Behind the memorial are moored the two ships used by the London Division of the Royal Naval Volunteer Reserve, HMS *Chrysanthemum* and HMS *President*.

On the northern side, between Carmelite Street and John Carpenter Street, is the Sion College, which was founded in 1630 near London Wall and moved to this site in 1886; the college contains a library of over 300,000 books, mainly theological. Next to Sion College is the City of London School for boys, founded by John Carpenter, a clerk to the City in the early fifteenth century. The school formerly stood in Milk Street, Cheapside, and was moved to this site in 1882.

Next to the City of London School is the huge building of Unilever House, the London headquarters of Lever Bros, the soap and detergent manufacturers. This site was formerly occupied by a large hotel called De Kuypers, later the Royal, but its business declined in the 1920s and it was converted to its present use.

Owing to the heavy traffic congestion at the junction of Blackfriars Bridge an underpass was constructed in 1967 to take traffic under the bridge to Queen Victoria Street.

VINE STREET EC3 (Crosswall) H3

Many of the City's wine warehouses are situated in this street, and it is from these that the name is derived.

VINTNERS PLACE EC4 (Upper Thames Street) D4

The Hall of the Vintners Company stands here, having occupied the site since 1357 when the first Hall was built on the site of the House of the Earl of Worcester. That Hall perished in the Great Fire of London, and was replaced in 1671 by another designed by Sir Christopher Wren. Wren's Hall was restored in 1823, but suffered badly in the bombing of World War II; it is now completely restored, and once again is used for the meetings and functions of the wine trade. In 1363 Sir Henry Picard, a former Lord Mayor, entertained no less than five kings at a banquet in the Vintners Hall, and today, whenever a toast to the company is offered, the members give five cheers. The Vintners, like the Dyers, are privileged to keep swans on the River Thames, and they distinguish theirs by marking the bills with two nicks: many years ago there were many taverns in the City whose sign was The Swan with Two Necks, a corruption of the swan with two nicks. The swan warden and members of the company go on an annual 'Swan Upping' expedition down the Thames to mark the bills of any cygnets belonging to the company.

VISCOUNT STREET EC1 (Fann Street) D1

Bridgewater House, the residence of the Earl of Bridgewater, occupied the whole of this area in the seventeenth century. In 1687 the house was destroyed by fire, and the Earl's two sons, Charles, Viscount Brackley, and the younger, Thomas, both perished in the flames (see Brackley Street).

WAITHMAN STREET EC4 (Pilgrim Street) C3

The street is named in memory of Alderman Robert Waithman, whose shop stood on the corner of Fleet Street and Ludgate Circus. Robert Waithman was a bustling Welsh politician who became Lord Mayor in 1823, was five times Member of Parliament for the City, and so famous that the corner of Fleet Street was known as Waithmans Corner. He died in 1833. Waithmans Street runs close to the line of the old City wall.

WALBROOK EC4 (Cannon Street) E4

The origin of the name of the River Walbrook is uncertain, but it seems probable that it flowed a little to the west of the street, on its way to the Thames, along the outside of the very first defensive wall erected by the Romans, which wall encircled an area bounded by Cousin Lane, Dowgate Hill and Walbrook on the western side, Cornhill and Leadenhall Street on the northern side, and Billiter Street and Mark Lane on the eastern side. The Walbrook was the main source of water in that early Roman settlement, and it existed well into the fourteenth century, when, like the River Fleet, it became polluted by the filth and rubbish of the City. It was almost completely covered in by the end of the fifteenth century.

The river rose in the marshy land of Finsbury, running south in line with the modern Curtain Road and Appold Street and flowing underneath Broad Street station to Bloomfield Street; it then crossed London Wall just west of All Hallows church. At this point iron culverts have been found about 18 ft below ground in the foundations of the old Roman wall; these culverts were built centuries ago to allow the river to flow through the wall unhindered. From here the river turned westward towards Lothbury where it flowed through the churchyard of St Margaret's and through the western corner of the Bank of England. The church of St Mildred's Poultry was originally built on the bank of the Walbrook (see St Mildreds Court). The river then headed for the Thames, west of Walbrook, through the Water Gate (see Dowgate Hill), and then into the Thames near Cousin Lane.

The northern end of the present street is occupied by the Mansion House, the residence of the Lord Mayor of London (see Mansion House Street). Just to the south of the Mansion House stands Wren's church of St Stephen Walbrook (see St Stephens Row).

The street was badly damaged during the last war, the whole of the western side being obliterated, and it was here in 1954, during excavations prior to the building of the present Bucklersbury House, that the ancient Temple of Mithras was discovered. The temple can now be seen in the forecourt of Temple Court in Queen Victoria Street.

Also destroyed in the bombing was Barge Yard, named in memory of the barges which sailed up the old River Walbrook in the thirteenth century; the yard stood at the northern end of modern Bucklersbury House.

WARDROBE TERRACE EC4 (Queen Victoria Street) C4
In the fourteenth century the residence of Sir John Beauchamp stood on this site, and when he died in 1359 the house was bought by Edward III and subsequently became the storeroom for all the royal clothing worn on state occasions. The house was destroyed in the Great Fire of London.

WARWICK LANE EC4 (Newgate Street) C3
In the fifteenth century the house of the Earls of Warwick

stood in what was then called Eldenese Lane. Richard Neville, the Earl of Warwick, lived in the house, and, according to John Stow entertained many of his 600 followers there (they were known to have consumed six oxen for breakfast). Warwick House was destroyed in the Fire in 1666.

Sir Christopher Wren built a fine headquarters for the Royal College of Physicians on the western side of the lane in 1674, but in 1823 the building was demolished and the College of Physicians moved to a new site in Trafalgar Square.

The whole of Warwick Lane was bombed in World War II and one of the few buildings to survive was the Hall of the Cutlers Company (on the western side), which, though badly damaged has been completely restored. The Cutlers, makers of fine knives and surgical instruments, built their first Hall in Cloak Lane in the early fifteenth century, and here they stayed until the end of the nineteenth century when they moved to the present site. The cutlery trade has now moved to Sheffield and the Cutlers Company concentrates on apprentices from the surgical-instrument trade, annually inspecting their work.

WATER LANE EC3 (Great Tower Street) G5

Before this area was obliterated in 1941 a narrow thoroughfare stretched from Great Tower Street to the eastern side of Wren's Custom House in Lower Thames Street. In medieval times the lane was called Sporiars Lane because it was inhabited by the City's spur makers, who pursued an important trade in those days when the horse was the main form of transport. The name was changed in the fifteenth century when a water gate was erected at the river end of the lane. Until 1968 a tiny portion of Water Lane remained on the southern side of Great Tower Street, but this, too, has disappeared now that a new road is being cut through the bomb-damaged area to connect Great Tower Street to Lower Thames Street.

WATERGATE EC4 (New Bridge Street) B4

Stands on the site of the water gate of the ancient palace of Bridewell, which was situated on the western bank of the River Fleet (see Bridewell Place).

WATLING STREET EC4 (Queen Victoria Street) D3

Watling Street is one of the oldest thoroughfares in England, having been constructed by the Romans to run from Dover to South Wales. The road traversed Roman and Saxon London from London Bridge to Holborn, following the line of modern Oxford Street, to Marble Arch, where it met another Roman road that ran from a point near Westminster Bridge, across the site of St James's Park to the Edgware Road, parts of which, even today, are called Watling Street.

The Saxons are said to have given the route its first name when they called it Atheling Street, meaning Noble Street, and Watling Street is a corruption of that name. The only portion of the old Roman road remaining in the City is the stretch between St Paul's churchyard and Queen Victoria Street.

At the junction of Watling Street and Budge Row stood the church of St Antholin, which dated from the twelfth century and was destroyed in the Great Fire. Wren rebuilt the church in 1682 but it lay directly in the path of the newly-planned Queen Victoria Street, and was therefore demolished in 1870.

The church of St Mary Aldermary, however, on the opposite corner, survived the demolition, and can still be seen at the corner of Queen Victoria Street and Watling Street. The church was the first in the City to be dedicated to the Virgin Mary, hence the suffix Aldermary, and was originally built in Saxon times; it was destroyed in the Fire of 1666, rebuilt by Wren in 1682, suffered considerable damage in 1941, and has since been completely restored.

Another of Wren's churches, standing at the western end, did not fare so well in the bombing, and was, apart from the tower, completely destroyed. The church, St Augustine with St Faith, was rebuilt by Wren in 1687 to replace an old church destroyed in the Great Fire. Until recently its tower stood, minus the steeple and blackened by fire, amid the rubble of what was formerly a thoroughfare called Old Change. A new steeple has been added, and the tower has been incorporated in the new Choir School for St Paul's cathedral.

Today the western end of Watling Street has been completely rebuilt, and a fine office block called Gateway House occupies the southern side.

WEST HARDING STREET EC4 (Fetter Lane) A3

The street was named after Mrs Agnes Harding who, in 1513, bequeathed the whole of this area to the Goldsmiths Company (see East Harding Street).

WEST SMITHFIELD EC1 (Giltspur Street) C2

Here stood the City's jousting ground, commonly called the Smooth Field; nobility gathered here in medieval times to see the country's finest knights in combat. It was on this plateau, on 15 June 1381, that the young King Richard II confronted Wat Tyler and his followers, the meeting ending when the Lord Mayor, Sir William Walworth, ran his sword through the rebel leader. Tablets on the wall of St Bartholomew's Hospital mark the site where terrible public executions took place throughout the centuries; in 1305 Sir William Wallace, leader of the Scots, was hung, drawn and quartered on this site. Another tablet marks the site of the sixteenth-century religious executions, when John Rogers, vicar of nearby St Sepulchre's, and several other protestant martyrs, were burnt alive on the orders of Queen Mary I. In 1849, during excavations for the fitting of new sewage pipes, a pile of blackened stones and human bones were found a few feet below ground, directly in front of the entrance to the church of St Bartholomew the Great.

From the twelfth century until its closure in 1855 the open land was used as a site for the great Bartholomew Fair, the City's famous annual revelry (see Cloth Fair).

For centuries the northern part of the Smooth Field was used as a live cattle market, known as the King's Market, and is described as a filthy quagmire, surrounded by at least thirty taverns where the City's ruffians gathered. It was closed in 1855 and in its place the present meat market, called the Central Markets was erected (see Central Markets).

WESTMORELAND BUILDINGS EC1 (Aldersgate Street) D2
The mansion of the Earls of Westmoreland stood on this site, one of the many noblemen's houses to be erected in Aldersgate Street; the buildings, however, are still in ruins after the wartime destruction.

WHITE HART COURT EC2 (Bishopsgate) G2
A famous Tudor tavern called the Olde Whyte Hart stood between St Botolph's church and what is now Liverpool Street. It was pulled down in the late nineteenth century to make way for the Metropolitan underground railway terminus, which was then called Bishopsgate but is now renamed Liverpool Street.

WHITE LION COURT EC3 (Cornhill) F3
The old White Lion was one of Cornhill's best-known taverns. It was destroyed by a fearful fire in 1765 which consumed most of the old wooden houses on the northern side of Cornhill.

WHITE ROSE COURT E1 (Widegate Street) G2
Named after the White Rose tavern which stood on this site, the White Rose was a favourite inn sign in the middle of the fifteenth century; it was meant to show support for Richard of York who had adopted the white rose as his emblem in the Wars of the Roses.

WHITECROSS STREET EC1 (Beech Street) E1

Large crosses in open country are frequently seen in Catholic countries, and in medieval times one such cross, painted white, stood at the northern end of this street, on the site now occupied by Whitbread's Brewery. Another cross, painted red, stood a little to the west of the white cross, and the lane leading to it was called Red Cross Street. Red Cross Street and the southern end of Whitecross Street were obliterated in the first air raid on the City in 1940, and the whole area is now being reconstructed, skyscraper blocks of flats and offices rearing up from the bombed sites.

WHITEFRIARS STREET EC4 (Fleet Street) B3

In the thirteenth century the street formed an entrance to the monastery of the Carmelite monks, who wore white habits and were therefore known as the white friars. The monastery, built in 1241, was founded by Sir Richard Gray, and occupied the whole area between New Bridge Street, Fleet Street, and the River Thames. It was dissolved in 1538 by Henry VIII. The privilege of sanctuary that the monastery enjoyed continued after the dissolution, and the whole area became a refuge for the thugs and villains of the City. Taverns and brothels sprang up in the narrow streets which had been constructed on the site, and the district was then called Alsatia; so infested did Alsatia become with thieves and prostitutes that an Act of Parliament was passed in 1697 abolishing the rights of sanctuary.

In a little courtway called Brittons Court, a portion of the old monastery can be seen in the cellar of what was formerly a house but is now part of the huge buildings of the *News of the World*, to whom written application to see the remains should be made.

In the seventeenth century, on the corner of Whitefriars Street and Fleet Street, stood the old watchmaker's shop of Thomas Tompion, who is described as the father of English clockmakers. He was buried in Westminster Abbey in 1713.

WHITTINGTON AVENUE EC3 (Leadenhall Street) F3

The avenue was named after Richard (Dick) Whittington, who bought the mansion of Sir Hugh Neville which, owing to its immense leaden roof was called Leaden Hall. Whittington then granted the mansion to the City Corporation, which in 1445 converted it into a granary; the mansion was later demolished and the site became the meat market known today as Leadenhall Market. Richard Whittington has been remembered by naming this entrance to the market Whittington Avenue.

Richard Whittington came to London as a boy of thirteen and was apprenticed to a Mercer. He eventually became a member of the Mercers Company, and later the City's most legendary figure, for in 1396, according to tradition, he was heading north up Highgate Hill with his cat, despairing at his fortune, when he heard the bells of St Mary le Bow, Cheapside, calling him back to become Lord Mayor of London.

Richard Whittington died in 1423 and is buried in the church of St Michael Paternoster Royal, College Hill. At the foot of Highgate Hill there is a monument to Dick Whittington, adorned by a statue of his cat.

WIDEGATE STREET E1 (Middlesex Street) G2

In the sixteenth century, when this area was open fields, pig farms were numerous and the wide gate spanned what was then known as Hog Lane, now Middlesex Street.

WINE OFFICE COURT EC4 (Fleet Street) B3

In the sixteenth century the office that issued licences to sell wine stood here; it was destroyed in the Great Fire of 1666.

In 1760 Oliver Goldsmith resided at what was then number 6, and here he wrote *The Vicar of Wakefield*.

The Cheshire Cheese, probably the City's most famous tavern, stands on the eastern side. The old tavern, which was the favourite rendezvous of Dr Johnson and his friends, is almost unchanged to this day; sawdust is still sprinkled on the floor of the tiny bars, the furniture is essentially eighteenth century, and in the summer the American accent is predominant. Wine Office Court still retains its eighteenth-century appearance, despite the bombing of Fleet Street in World War II.

WOOD STREET EC2 (Cheapside) D3

The origin of the name of this street is uncertain; wood was sold here during the days of the old Cheapside market, Sir Thomas Wood, Sheriff of London in 1491, lived here, and wooden houses were built in the street, despite the orders of Richard I that all new houses were to be built of stone.

On the corner of Cheapside stands a portion of the churchyard of St Peter Cheap, an old Saxon church destroyed in the Fire of 1666. In that churchyard can be seen the plane tree immortalised by Wordsworth in his 'Poor Susan':

> At the corner of Wood Street when daylight appears
> Hangs a thrush that sings loud, it has sung for three
> years,
> Poor Susan has passed by the spot, and has heard
> In the silence of morning, the song of the bird.

The plane tree and the churchyard were two of the survivors of the bombing of 1940.

Another church standing on the same side, near Gresham Street, was called St Michael Wood Street; it was rebuilt by Wren after the Great Fire but was pulled down in 1897 to make way for an office block. The head of James IV of Scotland was kept in the old church.

In the middle of the road, north of Gresham Street, can be seen the tower of the church of St Alban, one of the many churches rebuilt by Wren after the Great Fire; the church was destroyed in the bombing of 1940 and in reforming the area the tower has been left standing.

In recent years a new City of London police station has been erected on the eastern side of Wood Street, on the site of what was before the bombing Little Love Lane.

North of London Wall a plaque on the corner of St Alphage Gardens marks the site of the Cripple Gate, one of the main gates to the old City wall. The whole of this northern part of Wood Street was destroyed by the first bombs to fall on the City, on 25 August 1940 (see Fore Street).

WORCESTER PLACE EC4 (Upper Thames Street) D4

Worcester House, the riverside home of an Earl of Worcester, occupied this site; the Earl was a great collector of books, and part of his fifteenth-century collection can be seen today at Oxford University. The Earl was executed on Tower Hill in 1470 for showing allegiance to Edward IV during his quarrels with Warwick the kingmaker.

WORMWOOD STREET EC2 (Bishopsgate) F2

The old City wall ran along the northern side of this street and the land close to the wall was allowed to grow wild; among the many wild flowers and herbs growing there was the wormwood, a tiny herb used in medieval times as a woodworm killer.

The site of the Bishop's Gate which spanned the roadway between Wormwood Street and Camomile Street is marked by a plaque on the wall of Messrs Horne Bros.

WRESTLERS COURT EC3 (Camomile Street) G3

Named after a medieval inn called the Wrestlers which stood almost against the City wall, whose course runs through the foundations of the buildings on the northern side of Camomile Street.

Bibliography

Betjeman, John. *The City of London Churches.* 1967
Harben, H. A. *A Dictionary of London.* 1918
Hare, Augustus J. C. *Walks in London.* 1883
Loftie, W. J. *A History of London.* 1883
Smith, J. T. *Streets of London.* 1854
Stow, John. *A Survey of London.* 1598. Reprinted in Everyman edition
Times Book of the City of London, The. 1927
Walford, E. & Thornbury, W. *Old and New London Illustrated.* 1873